Earthly, Transcendental and Spiritual Logic

From Husserl's Phenomenology to Steiner's Anthroposophy

Scott Elliot Hicks

Other books available by the same author:

1. The Shattering Light of Stars

Cover art by Matt Sponenberg

2. The Resurrection of Thinking: Steiner's Anthroposophy and the Postmodernism of Badiou, Deleuze, Derrida & Levinas

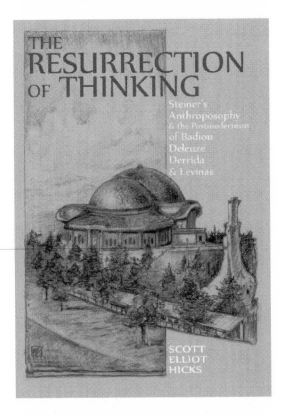

Cover and internal art by Aaron Butler

<u>Mottoes of this Work</u>

And I will pray the Father, and He will give you another Helper,
that he may abide with you forever – the Spirit of truth, whom
the world cannot receive, because it neither sees Him nor
knows Him; but you know Him, for He dwells with you and
will be in you.

(John 14)

***

Maria: "There is one region only in the spirit realm
In which there can be forged the sword
Before whose sight you [Ahriman] have to disappear.
It is the realm in which the souls of men
Form knowledge out of powers of reasoning
And then transform it into spirit wisdom."

(Rudolf Steiner, *The Soul's Probation*)

***

Mephistopheles: Not gladly do I reveal a loftier mystery—
Enthroned sublime in solitude are goddesses;
Around them is no place, a time still less;
To speak of them embarrasses.
They are the Mothers!

Faust [terrified]: Mothers!

Mephistopheles: Do you fear?

Faust: The Mothers! Mothers! Strange the word I hear.

Mephistopheles: Strange is it. Goddesses, to men unknown,
Whom we are loath to name or own.
Deep must you dig to reach their dwelling ever;

4

You are to blame that now we need their favor.

Faust: Whither the way?

Mephistopheles: No way! To the Unexplorable,
Never to be explored; to the Unimplorable,
Never to be implored. Are in the mood?
There are no locks, no bars are to be riven;
Through solitudes you will be whirled and driven.
Can you imagine wastes and solitude?

...

Mephistopheles: I praise you, truly, ere you part from me,
Since you understand the Devil, I can see.
Here, take this key.

Faust: That tiny, little thing!

Mephistopheles: Seize and esteem it, see what it may bring!

Faust: It's growing in my hand! it flashes, glows!

Mephistopheles: Will you see now what blessing it bestows?
The key will scent the right place from all others:
Follow it down, 'twill lead you to the Mothers.

(Goethe, *Faust*, Part 2)

***

If philosophy begins with a fact, then it places itself in the midst
of a world of being and finitude, and it will be difficult for it to
discover any path leading from this world to an infinite and
supersensible one. If, however, philosophy begins with an Act,
then it finds itself at the precise point where these two worlds
are connected with each other and from which they can both be
surveyed in a single glance.

(J.G. Fichte, *The Science of Knowing*)

Contents:

Preface

What is consciousness, perception, and life? Is the way that our memory works totally arbitrary, or is there a deeper meaningful organization? Can we see our ideas? Can we use our powers of awareness to track down the basic elements of our thinking and our consciousness at the moment of their birth? Rudolf Steiner and Edmund Husserl both spent their entire adult careers examining these questions and trying to answer them in new ways that had never been attempted before: by using the intense clarity and objective balance of modern scientific thinking and consciousness to uncover the roots of this human life and consciousness itself. In this way they walked down a different path than the psychologists on one side, and the neurologists and other hard scientists on the other. Their philosophical investigations took them beyond the limits of knowledge and the investigations of both the Kantians and the German Idealists from whom they learned so much. Husserl called his path of investigation, transcendental phenomenology, and Steiner named his, anthroposophy. Their paths were very different from one another but each of them provided valuable insights that can help to elucidate the issues at the bottom of consciousness studies and shine light on the deepest social problems and moral riddles of our own times.

In *Analyses Concerning Passive and Active Synthesis (1920/1921)*, Edmund Husserl imagines the fulfillment of the Goethean dream of reaching the realm of 'The Mothers,' where a final clarification of the sources and reality of all consciousness and its essential structures would be laid bare in warmth and brilliant light. He says:

> If one has learned to see phenomenologically and has learned to grasp the meaning of intentional analysis, if one has – expressed in the form of the Goethean myth – found the way to the mother of knowledge, to its realm of pure consciousness in which all being arises constitutively and from which all knowledge as knowledge of beings has to fashion its ultimate comprehensible clarification, then one will initially make the quite astounding discovery that those types of lived-experience are not a matter of arbitrary special features of an accidental life of consciousness, but rather that terms like perception, memory, expectation, etc., express universal essential structures, that is, strictly necessary structures of every conceivable stream of consciousness...formal structures of a life of consciousness as such, whose profound study and exact conceptual circumscription, whose systematic graduated levels of foundation and genetic development is the first great task of a transcendental phenomenology. It is precisely nothing other than the science of the essential shapes of consciousness as such, as the science of maternal origins.[1]

---

[1]APAS, pp 365-366

In this book, I would like to follow a rich and robust path into the bosom of a maternal human knowledge, filling up the empty clothes of Husserl with new life, and opening a gateway for real spiritual Imagination, Inspiration, and even Intuition to shine into our work from the spirit of Anthroposophy. Then I would like to supercharge it and offer it back again to the spiritual worlds, full of fruit harvested from our earthly life. In this way, the present book can provide a path to mutual nourishment from the earth to the heavens, and an opportunity to renew the soul and spiritual life of the human being and the earth. This will create a supersensible pulse between the sun and earth, in which we can cooperate with the Gods, if they so wish it. And they do wish it! Phenomenology itself can then wake up to a new and fuller life, an objective spirit of the air, a living sensible and supersensible organ within the newly born and enlivened body of humans on the earth, who are now becoming solar and cosmic in a moral way. By this, we can expand and enliven the spark of 'intellectual intuition' which began with Fichte jumping over the borders created by Kant, and extending through the self-awakening of the Concept in Hegel, and penetrating the strict forms of scientific logic and mathematics with the depth of inner soul in Bolzano and Lotze and continuing up to Brentano and Husserl. This element living in the pulsing memory of the world mind can be developed further now, resurrected in human consciousness and its sap can flow and grow in the wakening working body of the Christ Event that is happening in the body of the new solar earth in which we live. I offer my work, which is the creation

of this new spirit-organ of phenomenology, a new
etheric oculus of mind-heart-will, as the smallest gift
to the Michaelic school in the spiritual world. They
are working to awaken the spirits of thinking that
have died on the earth to new supersensible life again
– and this time, we can contribute an
anthroposophically awakened and created
consciousness of a new type of human to our shared
work. In this way, the karma of German
investigations into logic, idealism, and
phenomenology, can become streams of life that can
nourish the great mother of Anthroposophy herself.
Through this meeting, perhaps a more energetic co-
working can occur in the 21st and 22nd centuries and
beyond between the work of the humans in the
Michael school, the spirit of Rudolf Steiner himself,
and the work of the phenomenologists, idealists, and
the old school of Chartres being reborn. I hope that
my work can contribute to this resurrection of
Anthroposophy herself.

One can do fine research in America into the
realm of this motherly knowledge which humans are
seeking in our ages. In America we have a special
relationship to the electro-magnetic and reproductive
forces that surge down in the interior of the earth.
These powers work inside each of our souls and
bodies. In reference to Goethe's hint about the
spiritual role of 'the Mothers,' Steiner says:

> In his connection with Faust, Mephistopheles, in
> his capacity as an ahrimanic force, belongs to our
> world of the senses, but as a supersensible being.

11

He has been transplanted. He has no power over the worlds into which Faust is now to be transplanted. They really do not exist for him. Faust has to pass over into a different state of consciousness that perceives, beneath the foundation of our world of the senses, the never-ceasing weaving and living, surging and becoming, from which our sense-world is drawn. And Faust is to become acquainted with the forces that are there below.

The 'Mothers' is a name not without significance for entering this world. Think of the connection of the word 'Mothers' with everything that is growing, becoming. In the attributes of the mother is the union of what is physical and material with what is not. Picture to yourselves the coming into physical existence of the human creature, his incarnation. You must picture a certain process that takes place through the interworking of the cosmos with the mother-principle, before the union of the male and female is consummated. The man who is about to become physical prepares himself beforehand in the female element. And we must now make a picture of this preparation that is confined to what goes on up to the moment when impregnation takes place — all therefore that takes place before impregnation. One has a quite wrong and materialistically biased notion if one imagines that there lie already formed in the woman all the forces that lead to the physical human embryo. That is not so. A working of the cosmic forces of the spheres takes place; into the woman work cosmic forces. The human embryo is always a result of cosmic activity. What is described in materialistic natural science as the germ-cell is in a certain measure produced out of the mother alone, but it is a counterpart of the great cosmic germ-cell. Let us hold this picture in mind — this becoming of the human germ-cell before impregnation, and let us ask ourselves what the Greeks looked for in their three mothers, Rhea, Demeter and Proserpina. In these three Mothers they saw a picture of those forces that, working down out of the cosmos, prepare the human cell.[2]

Can we set aside our biases, limited viewpoints, and personal attachments to particular interpretations in order to experience the truth of reality directly? If we could somehow stand a little separate from our own normal and natural attitude, we might be able to more maturely, objectively, and with stoic equilibrium, meet nature and other people in a deeper and more clear and fundamental way. But do we have access to the inner truth and actual processes of our earthly society, our natural environment, and our local cosmos through the innate powers of our human existence in the first place? Each of us know that we can make errors in our judgment and in our thinking, but does that signify that our thoughts never connect with the living pulse of the world outside of us? Husserl and Steiner both would suggest that our thinking can in truth penetrate and open up and merge in a scientifically legitimate and accurate way with the world and the life outside of our skin. Ultimately Steiner and Husserl do not take an identical path to

---

[2] Steiner, GA 273, 2 Nov 1917

find epistemological and moral security in a true and living world beyond our personalities. Both of them do, however, rest their creative worldviews on the foundations of intuitive thinking which can demonstrate and stand on its own logical and ontological foundations. They both believe that human consciousness itself can be a tool to uncover its own essence, and that logical and strict thinking, trained with scientific rigor, can provide legitimate and sufficient evidence to secure the foundations of human knowledge and life.

In this book, I will not give a complete summary and interpretation of each of their worldviews. There are quite a few excellent books on Husserl in a variety of languages. The works of Cairns, Centrone, Derrida, Welton, Sokolowski, Fink, Ingarden, Bachelard, Levinas, and Lawlor are high quality. There are also a few books which can give an external but accurate overview of Steiner's project in a representational form. I have read some of them, but I am generally not a fan of secondary anthroposophical literature. I had my first inkling that consciousness continues after death in 1994, and I ran into phenomenology about the same time. Ever since then, I have only really appreciated authors or speakers when they directly demonstrate their knowledge by showing a transformation of consciousness in real time. I have always enjoyed following others into their new realms of expanded consciousness. Because I could see Ideas and concepts as real objects in the mind's eye from my early 20s, I always had a certain mistrust for authors or speakers who only talked <u>about</u> something, without simultaneously enacting it. Perhaps then you can understand why, after searching through the history of western philosophy and esotericism in my years in the Universities pursuing degrees in philosophy, I gravitated toward Husserl and Steiner. Happily, I was able to meet both thinkers in the classes and the libraries of Penn State University. Continental philosophy was also still very much alive at the University of Memphis in the 90s. I owe a great debt to many fine teachers who are too numerous to name. However, the only books that engage with the Spirit of Anthroposophy in a living way today that I can really recommend are those of Yeshayahu Ben-Aharon. He has also been my teacher, and we also share the same teacher in common. But as in my other works, such as *The Resurrection of Thinking* (2018), I will demonstrate a creative living process rather than a critique. I will not present an argument made of linguistic propositions, or a battle for supremacy crafted out of dead mental pictures. I am always working beyond the mental pictures or dead conceptual strata.[3] Of course, one must elaborate these concepts using everyday consciousness first, but then the meat of the experience lies in transforming these frozen and dead forces into something new, alive, and filled with soul and spirit. I am contributing a new leaf to the evolving conceptual artwork pulsing in the living being of organic knowledge as a whole. To read

---

[3] This is why I have omitted references in this book to the scholarly publications that try to link Husserl with mysticism or catholic theology in a totally external and theoretical manner.

this book, you have to become the book, because it is the new supersensible leaf. I have learned quite a bit by wandering through the sensible and supersensible leaves in the woods of Pennsylvania.

If you meet this book, you can find that the everyday experience of logical thinking by means of external rules and representations will be deepened and transformed in two ways: first, into directly-seen meaning forms in transcendental intuition and then into supersensible Imagination through crossing the threshold according to the Anthroposophical spiritualization of thinking. There is a giant gap between these two levels, however, and no linear path. In our demonstration of how to cross this gap, we will find that the logical rules of modus ponens, material implication, and so on, will become aspects of meaning-forms shown on the proto-light structure of eidetic seeing. But after we cross the gap, they will become alive and renewed as a moment by moment conversation with the wholeness of the spiritual world - where I am created, I am imagined, I am intuited by the Other. When we transform strict logical thinking into supersensible experience, we will gain life and wholeness but will lose none of the precision and objectivity. In this transformation of earthly logic into transcendental logic, and then into spiritual logic, we will experience the moments where we weave new threads of life into a new etheric earth, where we behold that the spirits behold the resurrection of transcendental idealism coming to life in our souls, and where we will experience how the angels live as our thinking. Through this resurrection of phenomenology and logic, we live, feel, and walk beyond Cartesian and Goethean limits, into the realms where the being of death is found living inside our heads, and where the Formless Spirit of thinking awakens to life in the wholeness of my cosmic-earthly body. This means we will step beyond 'I think therefore I am' and the sensible-virtual metamorphosis of qualitative forms. We will create new modes of moral-spiritual logic through the heart's spiritualized blood, and find how the Event of Christ's new appearance in the etheric can transform the nature of your Self altogether. We will discover the moments where logical propositions, judgments, syllogisms, and inferences can awaken in the realm of spiritual life, formative growth, and new wholeness. A birth of a new human thinking and reason takes place in the folds of the living plane of this book.

My job is to show the main wrestling match as it happens in the conceptual realm itself, not to describe it in a newspaper the next day. By the nature of this real battle and living struggle inside the life of thinking, I must also enter into the main event. I cannot remain a mere spectator. If you are interested in following the real action at the core of this book, you have to transform yourself and enter into the real drama also. It is addicting, but I think you will be able to get in and get out again safely. Do you want to join me on this sober adventure? Let's go!

Chapter 1 - Basic Introduction to the work of Rudolf Steiner (1861–1925) and Edmund Husserl (1859–1938)

Rudolf Steiner

Edmund Husserl

Rudolf Steiner and Edmund Husserl almost shook hands in Vienna in the closing years of the 19th century. They both lived in this wonderful city in 1881 and 1882. Husserl, the father of transcendental phenomenology, was completing his PhD in Mathematics at the University of Vienna. Steiner, the creator of Anthroposophy, was a student at the Technical University of Vienna (founded in 1815), but he occasionally attended lectures in philosophy at the University of Vienna as well. There, Steiner listened to the charismatic addresses of Franz Brentano and developed a life-long admiration for his work in descriptive psychology. Eventually this admiration would culminate in Steiner's extensive and delightful treatment of Brentano's thought in *Riddles of the Soul* (1917). His text offers fruitful techniques for conducting spiritual scientific research beginning from an investigation of the nature of cognition. We will use these techniques in chapter 8.

Brentano, whose most famous book is *Psychology from an Empirical Standpoint* (1874), also provided much inspiration for Husserl's phenomenology through his notion of the 'intentional relation' and his insights into the nature of the psyche. Steiner, who eventually received his PhD in philosophy in 1891, knew of Husserl and refers to him by name as well as to the 'Husserl School' in a passing way in a small number of places in his gigantic collected works (over 350 volumes). The references usually focus on Husserl's student, Max Scheler, who produced a phenomenological description of the essence of moral values, the emotions, and the experience of the ego of another person. Scheler attended some early lectures of Steiner, and met with Steiner a few times. Steiner seems to have preferred Scheler's work to Husserl's. He says of Scheler, "Every acute observer knows that it is not an inference by analogy but rather a direct perception that brings us awareness of another's ego. I think that a friend or associate of Husserl's school in Göttingen, Max Scheler, is the only philosopher to actually hit upon this direct perception of the ego."[4]

Although it is tempting to imagine Steiner and Husserl in their youthful 20s, sitting in the same hall of the University of Vienna listening to Brentano or arguing in the German language at a local café, there is no evidence that Steiner and Husserl ever met.[5] They were living in and around the area of Vienna for much of the 1880s. Husserl returned to Vienna once again to initiate his post-doctoral philosophical studies with Brentano in 1884, and Steiner tutored for

---

[4]*The Boundaries of Natural Science* (GA 322, lecture 7). Husserl tried to defend the notion of this analogical experience of the other person in the process of apperception. This is one of the weakest parts of Husserl's thinking as one can readily discover by wading through *The Cartesian Meditations.*

[5]They had other mutual acquaintances, such as the mathematician and philosopher, Georg Cantor, who served as an advisor on Husserl's post-doctoral committee. Cantor met Steiner in Berlin in 1900 to discuss the problem of the identity of Shakespeare, and said many kind things about Steiner in a letter to his son. See the *Beiträge (BE)* to Steiner's collected works, volume 114, <p. 54 – this style parentheses indicates the pages in the German edition>

the Specht family in Vienna, while he was writing his first books and editing Goethe's scientific works.[6] Two ships that passed in the night – such is life!

It is clear that Steiner closely studied the works of Brentano, Bolzano, Lotze, Scheler, and Dilthey (the sheer number of authors that Steiner mentions in his collected works is astounding), but he does not seem to have read much of Husserl. He at least owned both volumes of Husserl's most famous work, *Logical Investigations (1900)*.[7] Steiner was also well aware of the Neo-Kantian ideas and the Platonically-tinged transcendental analysis that had been developed in the Marburg school by thinkers like Cohen and Natorp, which would heavily influence the thinking of Heidegger, Cassirer and, to a lesser extent, Husserl.[8]

---

[6] Steiner also lived with his parents in a small apartment in the 16th century house in nearby Brunn in the early 1880s, from where he could travel by train to Vienna. There is a small museum dedicated to Steiner in the restored Heimat Haus which you can visit today. Through the kind invitation of Roland Rathner, I was able to retrace some of Steiner's footsteps in and around Vienna in August, 2019. Sometimes the tracing of such sensible-supersensible biographies can reveal surprising and unlooked for results.

[7] According to the list of the contents of Steiner's personal library in BE 114, but some pages in each volume were not yet 'cut open.' [I found some of Husserl's books in the same condition in Penn State's library around 2010!]. This obviously means that those pages were not read. Of course, I have quite a few books in my library which I have not yet read, so possession does not equal consumption.

[8] See GA 73a, where Steiner says in the context of a brief discussion after a lecture, "The Marburg School, which is primarily built on the very astute thinking of Hermann Cohen,

The following vague reference to Husserl's discussion of the Cologne cathedral suggests that Steiner had read at least book V of Husserl's *Logical Investigations*:

> The problem [of the difference between the pure stream of living thinking and the discontinuous elements of representational consciousness] is not actually touched upon [in Bergson and the Marburg School], and when it is raised, there is no consciousness of how to deal with it, not even in

has been rightly mentioned. Cohen has had the most significant influence on the Marburg School, and much can be traced back to his astute thinking. It can also be said that at a time when in German philosophy perhaps only Otto Liebmann was a truly perceptive thinker, outside of Marburg, the Marburg School actually had a disciplining effect and was educational for the development of a certain perceptive thinking. This Marburg school is now actually quite dependent on a certain one-sided development of Kantianism. One must say that the Marburg School came to this conclusion precisely through Cohen that thinking as such should not actually be regarded merely in its passivity, that it must be taken in its activity. And then, of course, the time period was not at all suitable to feel the inner validity of thinking in a way that lives outside the human being, as Fichte had done; but their modern view of thinking is more or less a subjective thinking, albeit with the claim of objective validity. Their subjective thinking has not really thought through to real objectivity, but they have deduced it. It was this kind of subjective activity of thinking that one arrived at. It was at a time when it was impossible to find out how the world process was actually objectively constituted, when it was hardly possible to look at anything other than this subjective operation of the activity of thinking." <p 499> (translation mine)

epistemological terms. Then again, not true, there is the direction of Husserl, but his approach is really not suitable for consideration. In my opinion, he is part of the school of Franz Brentano. With Franz Brentano there is the consistent fact that he is a sharply trained Aristotelian and a sharply trained Thomist, a good, thorough connoisseur of Thomistic thought, so that many things have passed to Husserl both from Aristotle and from Thomism. Of course, a modern philosopher like Husserl cannot easily admit this, but one can follow it in his psychology and in all that comes to light in him...I have to confess, when I wrote my *Riddles of Philosophy* in the new edition and tried to deal with these newer directions, I was always faced with the question: What should one actually do with Husserl? It is difficult to make something substantial out of his work no matter how hard you try. I have noticed so strongly how Husserl basically digs around in words, how he is also completely dependent on the content of words that are of secondary importance, in all his 'viewing of essences' and so on, and how he cannot come to a real view of even the simplest facts of consciousness. [*Es ist mir so stark aufgefallen, wie Husserl im Grunde genommen in Worten kramt, wie er auch bei aller seiner Wesensschau und so weiter ganz abhängig ist von dem sekundären Wortinhalt und wie er nicht zu einem wirklichen Schauen auch nur der einfachsten Bewußtseinstatbestände kommen kann*]. For Husserl, for example, it seems to be impossible to come to the conclusion what a difference there is between the picture of the Cologne Cathedral, which I have only noted in my memory down to the last detail, and the picture I have in front of me when I stand in front of the Cathedral and really look at it. So, I don't know where out of the whole structure of Husserl's philosophy a difference between these two pictures could be found to be essentially real. And if I'm not mistaken, even Husserl himself once used this picture of Cologne Cathedral in these two relationships, I think as an illustration. You don't actually get anything tangible out of his confusion running through all kinds of arguments.[9]

Notice that Steiner refers to Husserl's technique of '*Wesensschau*' or the viewing of the essences of ideas (which we will discuss throughout this book). This term was not introduced by Husserl until 1907, so this suggests that Steiner had read something besides the *Logical Investigations* or had heard of the general notion from other phenomenologists like Scheler.[10] Of course, by the time of Steiner's death in 1925, Husserl had published very little of his immense research (many of his works have now been published posthumously in about 40 volumes, with quite a few more to come). Really only the *Philosophy of Arithmetic, Logical Investigations* and *Ideas 1* were available for Steiner to read during his lifetime. It seems doubtful that Steiner read *The Philosophy of Arithmetic*. But did he read any the *Ideas* ? It is even possible that Steiner heard a lecture or two by Husserl, given that it is only 80 km from the center of the

[9] GA 73a, <pp 501-502> My translation
[10] On Husserl's connection with Aristotle and his development of the concept of 'the seeing of essences' refer to Hartimo's *Phenomenology and Mathematics*, p 117 ff.

Anthroposophical Society in Dornach to Freiburg, where Husserl taught from 1916 onwards.

Steiner does use the phrase 'scientifically rigorous' to describe Husserl, which may indicate that he had read the essay, *"Philosophy as Rigorous Science"* from 1911 and he also mentions that Husserl believes that the objects found in phenomenological research are necessary.[11] Steiner received lofty and

---

[11]Steiner says, "Und was von dem Ich, mehr streng wissenschaftlich, Husserl, der Philosoph, und dann etwas popular, namentlich in seinen neueren Aufsätzen, Scheler geschrieben hat, zeigt, dass die neuere Philosophie auf dem Wege ist, anzuerkennen, dass ein unmittelbares Bewusstsein auch etwas wissen kann von einem anderen Bewusstsein." GA 164, p 112. Steiner mentions Husserl on necessity here: "Yesterday we discussed how a deepening of our soul nature must be accompanied by a profounder grasp of concepts such as necessity. It was pointed out how decisive an influence on destiny a sense of the necessity in everything in existence, and the submersion of the individual in that necessity, could have for a person like Faust. But F. Mauthner says, "Necessity — What is it? Just a way of looking at things." He finds no reason to think of the element of necessity as existing objectively in things. In his opinion the stream of cosmic events bypasses human beings. People say that "the sun rose today, it rose yesterday and it rose the day before yesterday, so we assume that it will rise tomorrow and the day after tomorrow, and so on." They form the concept of necessity from these external thoughts about the regular succession of events, saying that the sun necessarily rises. But this necessity of theirs is subjective, just a human concept. And Mauthner makes the nice rejoinder to the philosopher Husserl, an exponent of the view that necessity is inherent in the nature of things, "If I only knew how necessity, a human way of regarding

important inspiration from the great figures of German Romanticism and Idealism (especially Goethe, Schiller, Hegel, Fichte, and Schelling), but these figures were much less important for Husserl.[12] Lotze and Bolzano were a much stronger influence on Husserl than they were on Steiner, although it is clear that Steiner knew a great deal of precise information about the work of both.[13] Nevertheless, Steiner was an expert on the major ideas and the development of

---

reality, could be made objective reality!" "If I only knew," is Mauthner's reaction. Mauthner, you see, lacks any possibility of understanding how something subjective could turn into objective reality. He's a queer kind of eurythmist, this Mauthner; he can never dance his way from the subjective into the objective because he has totally lost the capacity to involve himself in the inner choreography that leads from the subjective into the objective. And the reason for that is that we are not in a position to look for essential being at the characteristic place where the subjective element actually passes over into the objective realm." (GA 163, p 63). There may also be a reference to Husserl's notoriously convoluted and difficult writing style in Steiner's lectures to the early Waldorf teachers. At one point, Steiner compares a person's mode of speech to a book by either Husserl or Ruskin, about which the stenographic report is unclear. (GA 300b, p 73)

[12] Even though Husserl taught courses on Fichte's ethics, he never seems to have understood the close connection between the primary intuition in Fichte and the role of categorial intuition in phenomenology.

[13] Steiner mentions Lotze several times in his collected works and also owned four books by Bolzano (BE 114), whom he discussed many times as well (e.g. GA 65). To comprehend just how completely Steiner understood the living history of Philosophia, see *Riddles of Philosophy* (GA 18)

German philosophy in the 18th and 19th century, and was familiar with the early days of the phenomenological movement in a general way. It should also be mentioned that Steiner's knowledge of the world was not limited to reading in books. But in any case, I am not writing an historical account or trying to trace and locate trails of influence through textual comparison or larger cultural influences, so this ends my external overview.

Then why write a book today about these two worldviews which almost bumped into one another in the 19th century at all? Steiner himself does not exactly give the strongest endorsement of Husserl, and Husserl was certainly never interested in theosophy or anthroposophy, which was merely 'mysticism' to him. I believe that even if Husserl and Steiner had never almost met in their college days, their careful description of the subtle aspects of consciousness that we find in human thinking, memory, and sensation, their unparalleled analysis of the activity of philosophical intuition, and their elaboration of the realm of pure concepts would be enough to justify the research path demonstrated in this book. If we add together the totality of their work (close to 500 volumes, if we include Steiner's *Beiträge* and Husserl's unpublished manuscripts that are slowly seeing the light of day) the two of them penetrated more deeply into the nature of thinking, knowledge, and consciousness than anyone before or since.

But more than this, we also find interesting and curious parallels in their epistemological paths at various twists and turns. We are drawn to ask questions such as 'what is the relationship between Husserl's imaginative variation which leads to the vision of the eidos and Steiner's Imagination proper?' Or 'what is the connection between the data revealed in the phenomenological reduction in Husserl and Steiner's rigorous clairvoyant research into the nature of consciousness and thinking? Are they peering into the same lake?' For over a decade, I was convinced that they were indeed gazing into the same waters, but in 2009 I began to change my view radically after starting to work directly with Yeshayahu Ben-Aharon. His guidance in the Independent School of Spiritual Science and the Global Event College (where I am a faculty member) as well as his books, *The New Experience of the Supersensible, The Event in Science, History, Philosophy & Art*, as well as lectures from *Spiritual Science in the 21ˢᵗ Century* were essential in moving my understanding and experience of the riddles and difficulties involved to a deeper level. Intense struggles in the transformation of consciousness, thinking and the expansion of morality were necessary to reach the stage of wakefulness necessary to view the real nature of the difference between Steiner and Husserl. This work was also done with many friends, and was not just a solo effort. The difference between the two approaches is not a theoretical issue or one arising from scholarly minutiae. More importantly, the interpretation and experience of Anthroposophy itself depends on establishing this same vantage point. Ben-Aharon also wrote his doctoral thesis on the problem of the I in Husserl's phenomenology (unpublished and in

28

Hebrew). Our mutual interest in Husserl and Anthroposophy brought us together. This collaboration has been very fruitful and you can find evidence of it in this book.

As in my book, *The Resurrection of Thinking* (2018), I am concerned with clarifying, explaining, demonstrating, and teaching in a variety of different ways the unique nature of intuition in the field of human thinking. Husserl and Steiner were both experts in using this faculty. It is unfortunately the case that most people cannot yet awaken this faculty in clear consciousness, not even to the degree that Husserl was able to enact it. Steiner was able to infinitely deepen this faculty, until it emerged as a direct entering and living in the region of the Spiritual Beings by themselves, in a full-fledged Spiritual Intuition. By the end of the book I hope I will have sufficiently demonstrated that Husserl and Steiner are in fact **not** looking into the same waters, since Husserl never crossed the threshold fully to even begin Imagination proper, but nevertheless the process of clarifying and experiencing these differences can be extremely healthy, invigorating, and elucidating in the deepest cognitive and moral way. Husserl has left us with a powerful toolbox that we have to transform in a different direction.

If we can understand and directly perceive how the mental representation is formed through a process of unconscious paralysis and death in the realm of thought, we will have taken the first step in seeing why Husserl's project reached certain barriers that

Steiner was able to overcome. It is also thankfully now possible, due to the Spirit of our time, to be able to fully elevate and spiritualize Husserl's own work, so that its best parts can now serve as an entry point into the true spiritual worlds, provided we understand and follow the path I have outlined here. Spiritualizing Husserl's phenomenology is certainly not the only way to enter into the spiritual world today, but if the spark of Anthroposophy is added to it, there is indeed a way through. Furthermore, it is a rigorous and sober way, based on clear thinking and moral balance, and therefore appropriate for our time and our life as modern humans.

We will also see that Husserl and Steiner agree on some fundamental aspects concerning the nature of thinking, for example, that there is a numerical identity in the ideal objects which are at the foundation of our thinking, but that they function in numerically manifold judgments. In other words, there is only one concept of coffee in the entire world, and all people intuit the exact same singular ideal reality when they think of a cup of Joe.

I want to first help you understand the project as a whole and also introduce a bit of the fundamental insights found in Husserl. I am also assuming that you have a serious acquaintance with anthroposophy and the history of philosophy. If not, you may have a great deal of trouble in diving into the central activity of the work. I also think that the book, *The Wholeness of Nature,* by Bortoft could be read as a preparatory introduction to my book.[14] Where his book ends, mine begins. I could say the same thing about the works of Holdrege and Talbott coming out of *The Nature Institute*. I feel that the work of the *Global Event College* can be seen as the next rung on the ladder built by their work. Our work takes place in different dimensions, and the leap from their last rung to my first rung is a giant one, but it may be easier to understand what I am performing in this text if you first start to transform your thinking through various approaches to Goethean science.

Let us now begin by paying attention to the nature of our own thinking. Think about what you did yesterday. Everybody is vaguely familiar with the nature of thought, but in this study, we shall carefully examine and observe the activity of thinking itself as it happens. This does not only mean 'thinking about thinking.' Steiner can put our foot on the right path from the beginning: "Observation and thinking are the two points of departure for all spiritual striving of man insofar as he is conscious of such striving...Whereas observation of things and events, and thinking about them, are but ordinary occurrences filling daily life, the observation of thinking itself is a sort of **exceptional situation**. This fact must be taken into account sufficiently when we come to determine the relation of thinking to all other contents of

---

[14] You might also be able to make a link between Goethe's ideas and this book by reading the excellent article by Elke Weik, "Goethe and the Study of Life: a comparison with Husserl and Simmel," *Continental Philosophy Review*, 2017.

observation...It is characteristic of thinking that the thinker forgets thinking while doing it. What occupies him is not thinking, but the object of thinking which he observes."[15]

How do you understand the meaning of what you did yesterday? Let us set aside our preconceptions and old ideas about it. We may have been taught at one time that our ideas are copies of what we have seen or touched sometime in the past. If we believed in this notion, we might then imagine that a real physical and solid world exists outside of our skin and that just pale copies of these objects live in our heads. If this were so, we would organize and manipulate these pale images in order to think about elephants and strawberries that are not sitting in front of us in the room. But let us put all of these old ideas out of play and just watch what happens when we think about the events of yesterday. We might then notice that many times we do not even see a pale or vague image floating in our mind's eye when we think. Yet we still understand what we are paying attention to, whether it is a memory, a sound, or an object. Sometimes we use words or inner speech in our native language to accompany this process of meaning-elaboration, which either points to things we have seen in the past, or that refer to other times we have used the word or when others have used such words. We may have been taught in the past that language and logical sentences are signs or indicators for 'real sense objects' that exist outside of our bodies and heads. We

---

[15] GA 4, *The Philosophy of Spiritual Activity*

might then imagine that thinking is really a manipulation of language-strings or sentences in inner speech that we use to communicate with one another. For example, I use a combination of letters written in the Roman alphabet, 'c o p p e r' to refer to any actual experience of seeing or touching or working with that kind of metal. But let us once again set aside all of these ideas and presuppositions, and pay attention to just what is happening in our thinking moment to moment. Can we awaken this 'exceptional situation' that Steiner mentions? Watch the ebb and flow in your thinking as it searches for meaning, arranges ideas, creates new concepts, differentiates between different notions, and digs into the memories from yesterday. What is happening here?[i] Who is the thinker?

Let us now take a moment to focus on thinking's relationship to language. First, a sentence is not *understood* just because it has been spoken or written according to the grammatical rules of a particular language. The sound of the words is not equivalent to the meaning that is expressed through the words. This becomes obvious when you listen to someone speaking in a language you don't know. The thinker has to penetrate with consciousness into the realm where meaning reveals itself to reason and the understanding. We have to grasp or view the meaning of something in the invisible or non-sense-perceptible world of thought (thus the German word for concept, *Begriff*, indicates this gripping or grasping, as does the Latin root of 'concept,' *cum + captus*, indicating taking or capturing things and bringing them

33

together). In this way, we learn how to pass beyond the letters or the sounds in order to grasp or be gripped by the concept of something. An illiterate person glancing at the marks on the page of a book does not automatically grasp the meaning of the text. Notice how we usually forget what happens when we read: we penetrate with our active thinking into the virtual realm of concepts. Husserl says, "The word points away from itself and to the sense (or meaning) in normal discourse...Now we want to enter the broadest generality in which it is no longer a matter of words and statements, although it does concern, in an expanded sense, the production of meaning ('sense-givenness') and furthermore the distinctions between what is rational and irrational – distinctions that belong to the special theme of every logic."[16]

But how do I think of the concept of a bird building a nest or how do I understand what it means to place a reed into a clarinet mouthpiece? What happens in this willful activity of considering an idea and what it means? What do I dive into when I plunge into concepts? Where and how do I register the significance of what I understand? How do I hear and perceive the meaning of what I think in my interior at

---

[16] Husserl APAS pp 27, 28. I often will add the word 'meaning' to the translation where 'sense' has been used, to be clear of the difference between sense-perception (*Wahrnehmung*) and the sense (*Sinn*) or meaning (*Meining, Bedeutung*) of an idea. Husserl, of course, carefully distinguishes between *Sinn* and *Meinung*, but the issue is less important in our context, and it can be confusing for the English reader.

all? The ego that is directing the activity of thinking normally possesses an immediate comprehension of the meaning of the thoughts or propositions that it consciously generates inside, but rare cases may also occur in which someone repeats a phrase in inner speech without really understanding the meaning of the linguistic string. One might imagine that high school students memorizing Shakespeare could verify this experience. Sometimes in the morning, I realize that I have been thinking over a problem even before I consciously realize that I am awake. My soul uses language to think through the problem without the self-conscious I necessarily even being present. However, this rare case only underscores the fact that the expression of meaning is separate from a coherent sentence in a particular language. It is also true, that one's understanding of the meaning of a sentence evolves over time, so that you understand many more concepts and subtleties in Tolkien, Faulkner, Frank Herbert, Patrick O'Brian, Goethe, or Walt Whitman's writings than you did when you read them in your 20s or 30s and so on. Of course, neurological and psychological investigations may have something important to tell us about how thinking is related to our biological and organic processes, but at this point we will ignore their findings.

It can also become clear to the investigator that meaning is not only something different than a string of words or sounds, but that meaning, when examined meticulously, can be traced to a sphere of activity that stands outside the operations of ordinary language. *Thinking's unfolding blooms in a substance before my native language takes hold of it.* Husserl says, "When a thematic act is attached to words, what is meant in the act is called the sense of the word, or even, its significance (*Bedeutung*) because the word signifies (*deutet auf*). But independently of the fact whether an act has such a function of lending words significance, it has in itself a sense or meaning-content. Accordingly, we must liberate the concept of sense from its relation to expressions."[17] This does not just mean that basic grammatical categories exist as a proto-structure (as in Chomsky) or that neurological patterns predetermine and underlie all thinking (as in Churchland's work). *It means instead that the self-revelation of a concept occurs in the opening of a viewpoint that instantly reveals an aspect of the life and essence of the content of the concept.* The activity of the I AM is also different from this conceptual unveiling on the flowing concept plane. It is the Actor who produces and arranges its activity. As Steiner says, "It is the I itself, standing within thinking, that observes its own activity."[18]

Let us go deeper. For example, the pulsing life of a Red-Tailed Hawk is revealed inside the direct grasping of its concept (which happens before language, but) within a coherent idea that can be only partly expressed in a language or in a single mental image. Every possible perception of the colors of a hawk or the direction that this one is flying right now

---

[17] Husserl, APAS p 33, translation slightly modified
[18] *The Philosophy of Spiritual Activity*, chapter 3, addendum to the 1918 edition

in the sky, are connected to the invisible concept of the hawk that is thinkable in human minds. As Goethe recognized, the reality of the world as a whole is partly sensible or perceptible outwardly and partly viewable in the realm of concepts or inwardly. Goethe was skilled at tracing how the self-transforming 'fluid' of life pushed out into color, and disappeared into viewable idea once again. The living essence of all that a hawk can become, can be partly shown in colors, motion, sensations, and sounds that we can perceive with our senses, but another aspect of the becoming of the hawk is only revealed to our *capacity to grow a concept* out of its living essence in the invisible world of thought. This complex idea, which blasts the Kantian limits out of the water, is described by Steiner in this way, "Place the plant before you. In your soul it connects itself with a definite concept. Why should this concept belong to the entire plant any less than leaf and blossom? You say – the leaves and blossoms are there without the presence of a perceiving subject; the concept, however, does not appear till a human being confronts the plant. Quite true. But leaves and blossoms appear on the plant only if there is soil in which the seed can be planted, and light and air in which the leaves and blossoms can unfold. In just this way does the concept of the plant arise when a thinking consciousness confronts it."[19] In their thinking, humans are concept-growing-soil. At the deepest level, the light from the archetypes in spiritland pass through the activity of sensing soul light in the moods and duties of the angels as they

---

[19] *The Philosophy of Spiritual Activity*, chapter 5

perceive us. Their harmony, wisdom, and love in the world flows through every act of thinking.

Therefore, the concepts at the basis of linguistic communication are themselves more than words, more than sound. Simply put, the ideas we experience in thinking contain more reality than can be expressed through ordinary language. They are events of unfolding meaning to the supersensible eyes, heart and hands of a self-conscious thinker. Indeed, you can train yourself to think with all parts of the etheric body, including the etheric fingers, which stretch out like thinking roots in the spiritual life-world. Goethe and Steiner go further than Husserl in this regard, but nevertheless Husserl was knocking on the first door that opens onto spiritual science. His three important pathways to this door were 1) a moment by moment tracing of consciousness in perception, time-flow, and thinking; 2) seeing ideas; 3) and the technique of imaginative variation. One can recognize his kinship with Goethe and Steiner by examining these three approaches to authentically lived and experienced Anthroposophy. For example, Husserl makes the following remarks about the pre-linguistic field of consciousness that undergirds thinking:

> It is impossible to understand what thinking is (which is a highly built-up accomplishment) in the specific sense in order to be able to be expressed in language and universal words and in order to provide a science, a theory, if we do not go back prior to the thinking, back to those acts and accomplishments that make up the most expansive part of our life. For not only does a

pre-theoretical life reside in this expansiveness, but a pre-linguistic life as well, one that immediately ceases to be in its original, primitive peculiarity with every expression. And thus, I set the task of our further lectures to open up this expansive, great world of the interiority of consciousness. [20]

Note that here Husserl refers to the life of consciousness as a whole, which includes every minor sensation, perception, memory, the experience of time, anticipation, forgetting, moving the attention, as well as the experience of other people and the I. In other words, he is interested in both perception and thinking as they are included in the wholeness of life. He recognizes that our faculties are both creative and receptive in our conscious life. We must actively join concepts together in a logical process when we try to solve a problem by thinking about it (he associates this with 'active synthesis'). But certain aspects of our daily life flow on without our conscious control, such as the stream of time and memory, which seems to be 'passively constituted' (or 'passively synthesized'). Thus, Husserl's work is not only concerned with the viewing of essences in categorial or conceptual intuition, but also with the flow of perception and will movements that unfold in sensation. In this way, he learned a great deal from the careful scientific psychological and 'noetic' analyses of Brentano.

---

[20] APAS p 32

Chapter 2 – To See or to Be Seen? What is Ideation, Eidetic Seeing, or the Viewing of Essences?

Cyrtoidea from Haeckel's *Artforms of Nature*

Husserl describes the nature of phenomenology like this:

> It was only with phenomenology that we first had avenues of access, methods, and insights that make possible an actual theory of science, namely, through its radicality in going back to the consciousness of the production of meaning (or 'sense-giving') and the whole of conscious life. It is phenomenology that seriously inquires back from the ready-made propositions, theories, to thinking consciousness and to the broader nexus of the life of consciousness in which these formations are constituted; and it inquires back, going still more deeply from all types of objects of thought as the substrata of possible theories, to experiencing consciousness and its essential characteristics which make the experiencing accomplishment intelligible. It has allowed us to see in a presuppositionless manner the feature of intentionality as the very feature that makes up the fundamental essence of consciousness...making intelligible how objectivity as a true being of every kind is shaped as an accomplishment in the subjectivity of the life of consciousness.[21]

The simplistic abbreviation that is often used to introduce the basic idea of intentionality in phenomenology is that consciousness is always

---

[21] Husserl APAS p 31 (translation slightly modified)

directed toward something. In other words, consciousness is always 'consciousness of.' I am conscious of the pain in my foot, or I am conscious of my wife's voice. It was through Brentano's work that Husserl first recognized this primary feature of his world of interiority: that of the *intentional relation.* Brentano distinguished the experience of something *physical* from the experience of something *psychical,* by recognizing the fact that the inner processes of mental representation, judgment, and affectivity always refer beyond themselves to some object. I am concerned about my mother's well-being, for example. My anxious thoughts and feelings (which are obviously psychological) refer to her. After calling her, I make the judgment that she is no longer ill. As Steiner said above, we usually ignore thinking altogether, and only pay attention to what we are thinking about.

According to Brentano, physical phenomena do not possess this relation to the meaning and reality of something outside of their sphere. For example, the green of the leaf that I see does not refer to something else, it is the pure experience of green existing and showing itself. It exhausts its intensity in its own expression. But if I experience that I like the shape of the leaf, I am in the region of the 'intentional relation,' and therefore in the psychological realm. It is similar to the way that a financial instrument must be backed by something, while a commodity contains its own value. Likewise, for Brentano the experience of space does not refer to anything else in its function as a container for movement and objects, so it is not a mental state, but a physical one. The experience of moving through space does not point to another object outside of itself like a symbol. Space is like a pure commodity. But my opinions about the elections are psychological elements in my mind. It seems clear that the elections are happening in the world, not in my mind, and my thoughts and feelings only point to them. Whereas the experience of color, sound, and space are in some sense fully unfolded in their external and self-subsistent existence. In contrast, my feelings are always about something else, they refer to something else by means of an 'intentional relation' that I hold in my mind and soul or psyche. Space and color are not 'about' something else, in Brentano's estimation.[ii] Thus, I maintain an intentional relation to what I think about, to what I feel, and to what I make judgments about.

Husserl takes up Brentano's notion, calling it *Intentionality*, and develops it throughout his life work, indicating that when one turns the attention toward the processes and objects of mental life in clarity of focus, one can minutely investigate the pure features of consciousness in a strict scientific manner. Husserl starts to investigate just how my mental processes unfold in the process of thinking and understanding. He calls this new world of the interiority of consciousness, the region of the 'irreal,' as opposed to the natural sense of an external world that we perceive as 'real.' That does not mean that our mental images and inner speech are illusions, but Husserl wants to carefully point out the differences between the two worlds, and also wants to temporarily suspend judgments about the actual existence of the meaning-objects that appear inside our conscious thinking and knowing. To suspend belief in the natural attitude, requires him to perform the epoché [bracketing off the natural world and our traditional ideas about it] or the 'phenomenological reduction.' According to Husserl, we can find the true essences of all the things we know and encounter in the world in this irreal intentional realm.

Let us go more deeply into what Husserl means by pure essences and how we gain access to them through his method by tracing his descriptions in *Ideas I:*

> Experiencing or intuition [*Anschauung*] of something individual can become transmuted into eidetic seeing or ideation [*Wesenserschauung*], which is to be understood not as an empirical possibility, but as an essential potentiality. What is seen when that occurs is the corresponding pure essence or Eidos...The essence (Eidos) is a new sort of object. Just as the datum of an individual intuition is experienced as an individual object, so the datum of eidetic intuition is a pure essence...Seeing an essence is also precisely intuition, just as an eidetic object is precisely an object...Empirical intuition or, specifically, experience, is consciousness of an individual object...in quite the same manner, intuition of an

essence is consciousness of something, an 'object.'[22]

The basic difference to understand and experience at this juncture is between empirical perception and ideal intuition. What Husserl means is that we can perceive the colors and form of an individual pineapple, as we view it from one side. This process reveals sense impressions and we grasp it in our consciousness; in this way it is an empirical intuition of an individual object. But at the same time, we also connect the sense impressions of this object with the concept of a pineapple in our thinking. This understanding of the concept is conscious, or at least partly conscious, and is a conceptual intuition or a seeing into the realm of meaning. But the normal grasping of the category of pineapples in thinking, or the seeing of a mental picture of this particular pineapple as an individual in the mind's eye is not yet ideation or eidetic viewing. The viewing of essences only fully reveals itself, when I can self-consciously penetrate behind the individual mental picture to perceive the essence of any fruit whatsoever. This is not a process of abstracting or generalizing with pale words or mental images after grabbing and looking at a wide variety of fruit at various times in the supermarket.

Husserl is, on the contrary, describing a new kind of thought object, which is seen in its wholeness outside of any of my personal psychological elements.

---

[22] *Ideas I,* pp 10 - 11

45

This is why Husserl describes his phenomenology and his logic as 'pure.' It is purified of any connection with material causality, from connection with normal ideas of natural existence, and indeed purified from any personal limitations in how my psyche might receive the content of this categorial intuition. Another person can look at the colors of an apple along with me, but another person cannot use the same eyes to view the concept of any fruit whatsoever as a new kind of object in the thinking sphere. One needs the mind's eye for this, the thinking and understanding-eye of intuition. This means that I do not view the other person's mental activity with external perception, which is self-evident. My eyeballs don't see my friend's memories. Nevertheless, we both can think the concept with our capacity to reach into the world of pure concepts and categories. This is eidetic intuition and there are indeed various qualities that express themselves in this viewing of meaning that are very different from our sense experience of seeing an individual pineapple from one side. The morphology of the Eidos is different than the particular shape of that pumpkin in front of me. The Eidos has a flexible wholeness or a dynamic virtuality that is not found in the eye sockets of the jack-o-lantern. If you imagine that the *Cyrtoidea* illustrated by Haeckel were flowing with meaning light and in continual flashing motion, this would give you an approximation of how the essences appear in phenomenological intuition.

Furthermore, what makes this a new realm of activity, which demonstrates that it is different from sense impressions and abstractions, is that these concept constellations have different qualities, shapes, connections, and features than any perception of an individual apple hanging on the tree. This demonstrates to one who views them, that these *eide* (the plural of eidos, the Greek word for Idea, that Husserl selected for these essences) are definitely not generalizations, hypostatizations, abstractions, or hallucinations. This is what Husserl means when he calls them 'original.' They have an aspect that only belongs to them, and they belong to the deepest inner aspect of all beings. They are rich prototypes. Husserl paid more attention to the essences of features of logic, category, and ontological regions, rather than the essences of flowers and mammals, but his research method of Ideation shares a connection with Goethe's in its partial penetration into a Typus or Arche-typal Imaginations. The essences are not copies of things I have touched in the past and they are also not frozen platonic Ideas. Indeed, the experience of the Idea in ancient Greek times was much different than ours, as Steiner points out.[23] I have investigated and used

---

[23] "In the epoch described here the thought-life is still essentially different from that of modern times. The Greek thinker does not draw up thoughts from the depths of his soul, but thought is revealed to him just as external sound or colour is revealed to modern man. The Greek perceives the thought; he perceives it from outside and when we speak of Greek philosophy we must not speak of such a mode of thinking as is normal today, but of thought-perception. Thus in the first period we are concerned with *thought-perception*. Plato and Aristotle did not think in the way the modern philosopher thinks, they thought as today we see, perceive. They looked out into the world, as it were, and perceived the thoughts which they expound to

Husserl's methods for decades and can confirm his findings in regard to Ideation. Ideation is not 'metaphysical speculation' but an actual experience that can be described soberly and scientifically. Its products are also not drug dreams or visionary mystical experiences on the other side. The seeing of essences is more gentle and subtle than the psychotropic art of Alex Grey or Amanda Sage, but it is also way more vivid than Wittgenstein's arid investigations. It must also be carefully distinguished from the Imaginative capacity of Goethe and the World-shifting etheric cognition of Steiner (which is still only a small part of Steiner's accomplishments). It is unfortunate that even some very prolific Husserl scholars, do not perceive the real nature of his fundamental discovery. I place J.N. Mohanty into this category as a prime example. Of course, I find much of the work of Mohanty to be intelligent, penetrating,

---

us in their philosophies just as much as one perceives a symphony. They are thought-perceivers. The world reveals to them a thought-work; that is the essential character of the Greek thinker. And this perception of the thought-work of the world was brought to the highest pitch of perfection by the Greek thinker. If the philosophers of today believe that they understand what Plato and Aristotle perceived as a universal symphony of thoughts, that is only due to a childish stage of the modern philosopher. The modern philosophers have a long way to go before they can fully grasp what Aristotle represents as Entelechy, what he gives as the members of the human soul nature — Aesthetikon, Orektikon, Kinetikon etc. The inner activity of thinking, where one draws the thoughts out of oneself, where one must make subjective efforts in order to think, did not as yet exist in Greece." Steiner, GA 161, 10 Jan 1915

and valuable. But Mohanty's interpretation of Husserl is barely different than the main dispute which existed between Schiller and Goethe: the archetypal plant was a living idea that Goethe could inwardly perceive, but Schiller did not possess the faculty to see it. He therefore supposed that Goethe was merely projecting words onto a black screen.[24] Husserl himself describes the present state of humans in regard to their intuitive self-consciousness pretty well:

> Blindness to ideas is a kind of blindness in the soul [*Seelenblindheit*]. Because of prejudices [projected representations functioning in judgment = *Vorurteile*], one becomes incapable of bringing what one has in one's field of intuition [*Anschauung*] into one's field [of conscious thinking] or judgment. The truth is that all human beings see ideas, essences, and see them, so to speak, continuously. They operate with them in their thinking; they also make eidetic judgments,

---

[24] We still find the same basic misunderstandings which contaminate and obscure Husserl scholarship today. Unfortunately, the academic publishers and journals keep accepting articles about Husserl whose authors do not experience the first basic step of his intuitive procedure. A prime example is the article "Husserl's Logical Grammar." Ansten Klev - 2018 - *History and Philosophy of Logic* 39 (3):232-269. Klev has spent countless hours reading through 10 volumes of Husserl's posthumous writings and lecture notes on Logic, but he is not clear about the basic experience that underlies all of Husserl's writings: the intuitive seeing of the ideal world. This is not meant as a personal criticism, but as symptomatic of the overall trend.

except because of their epistemological viewpoint, they interpret them away.[25]

I have seen this unfortunate phenomenon play out in many different discussions and published arguments over the years – in the high school classroom, in philosophy conferences, in books and journals, as well as in 'anthroposophical' study groups and publications. People generally replace the experience of the concept grasped in the faculty of intuition with a representation formed unconsciously in the head. Even those who have some inkling of seeing objects in the mind's eye, really only focus their attention on this dead mental image or linguistic placeholder rather than toward the far-reaching, pulsing, opening of the vast field of concepts on the provisional concept plane far beyond the head.[26] In fact, many people only think in vague images, feelings, and strings of words, and are really only conscious of perceptible objects in the outer world. Husserl goes on to say how theoretical prejudice makes it very easy to dismiss what appears spontaneously in the eidetic seeing. The essences that appear in intuition are not created like mental images

---

[25] *Ideas I*, <p 41>

[26] The provisional concept plane where Husserl's activity is located is not yet the full virtual plane of Deleuze's activities, which is also not the fully etheric world of Steiner's investigations. When seen from all sides, these regions do overlap in many ways, however. Only the moral leap can transform the experience of the provisional concept plane into etheric cognition, as I described in my text, *The Resurrection of Thinking*.

in the mind's eye, but they appear as objectivities in some sense 'outside' of it. Concepts live outside the psychological. He says, "To designate [a cardinal number] as a psychical formation is therefore countersense, an offense against the meaning of arithmetical speech, which is perfectly clear, discernible, at any time, and therefore which precedes all theory. If concepts are psychical formations then those affairs, such as pure numbers, are not concepts. But if they are concepts [*Begriffe*], then concepts are not psychical formations [*psychischen Gebilde*]. As a consequence, one needs new terms, if only to resolve ambiguities as dangerous as these."[27]

Because of these problems of terminology, Husserl began to use the term 'noema' to refer to the individual meaning-element that is revealed in seeing concepts. It probably didn't help much. These ambiguities have also resulted in the total misinterpretation of all of Steiner's works, whether epistemological or anthroposophical. If one cannot experience intuition as the grasping of a new region of thinking beyond the personal soul boundaries, one can never find the way to living thinking or to Anthroposophy itself.[28] Husserl was half-way there. His limitations in certain areas have been finely pointed out by Levinas and Derrida, for example, but it is also necessary to first perceive his radical

---

[27] *Ideas I*, <42>

[28] Of course, Anthroposophical study can take us quite far, if we open the veils of our normal comprehension. For more on this, see *Outline of Esoteric Science*'s final preface.

achievement accurately before moving beyond it. I do not believe that Heidegger himself was capable of seeing essences with the clarity of his teacher. Therefore, his early Dasein-analytic is more structural and linguistic rather than eidetic.

Husserl suggests that, when one contemplates the accomplishments of conferring and realizing (or 'fulfilling') meaning in the world of interiority, one discovers intellectual objects that are not the outcome of a relationship of psychological events with external, physical objects: "On the contrary, we are concerned with experiences in their essential purity, with pure essences, and with that which is involved in the essence 'a priori,' in unconditioned necessity."[29] This

---

[29] Husserl, *Ideas I.* 1962. p. 108. (§ 36) "We must, however, be quite clear on this point that *there is no question here of a relation between a psychological event – called experience (Erlebnis) – and some other real existent (Dasein) – called Object –* or of a *psychological connection* obtaining between the one and the other *in objective reality.*" Morrison states, "Husserl warns that there are two errors that must, above all, be avoided. The first is the representational theory (*Bildertheorie*), according to which the physical thing is 'outside' conscious{ness} and its representatives (*Bilder, Vertreter*) are 'in' consciousness. The second error is that the intentional object is immanent, i.e., is a sign (*Zeichen*) or representation...The intentional object is not an 'internal representation' and the external thing is not something 'represented.' Rather, the intentional object is the transcendent, external object." Morrison, "Husserl and Brentano on Intentionality." *Philosophy and Phenomenological Research*, Vol. 31, No. 1 (Sep., 1970) p. 43.

intuitive method is 'transcendental phenomenology.' He is concerned with expanding or uncovering the category of 'any object whatsoever' as a real thought, that I can grasp and dive into with the arm of my mind which simultaneously moves into, opens up, and grasps the meaning of anything in thinking. One can grasp and verify the precise meaning of Husserl's ideation or eidetic viewing if one can perceive in the thinking sphere, or on the first or provisional concept plane, the fluctuating potentiality or virtuality of any object whatsoever. If one can intuit this with full saturation, as if one has completely dived into the water of the lake, then one can awaken the self-conscious faculty of the viewing of essences that Husserl describes. In a sense, if this faculty is awakened by penetrating to the seeing of the category of any object whatsoever, the same moment of wakeful intuition that Fichte always describes is simultaneously awakened. As Fichte says, there is only one individual intuition which is active everywhere. (We could progress one step further, and with devotion enter the real threshold to the spiritual world at this point, and then open the gap which lets the light shine in from the spiritual world, where then the spiritual self is revealed inside this intuition of the I. This is how Steiner's work can deepen Husserl's work at every point. It is one of the little keys. But we will only note this here in passing and discuss it later).

Husserl also notes that it is not necessary to first look at a cucumber at the farmer's market before I can intuit the essence of any vegetable whatsoever, or view the rules that govern the flowering of any plant

53

whatsoever. He suggests that one can pass directly from an imagination of a cucumber or a circle into the moment of full intuitive seeing. He notes that the process of intuiting the essence and seeing the individual image of the same subject-matter in the mind's eye are present at the same time, and one can shift between them freely. But one can only view with full saturation one aspect or the other. Often the imagination is called 'phantasy' in the translations of Husserl's writings into English (as for example in his lectures and notes from 1898 to 1925, *Phantasy, Image Consciousness, and Memory*, [Springer, 2005]). Consider any judgment about the relationship of the size of angles when two lines cross each other. I need only imagine one instance to grasp the complete rule (Fichte also makes this point). Husserl says that the viewing of axioms or general principles in mathematics or in physics is:

> ...A seizing upon essences; and this seeing too, like the eidetic intuition which makes essences into objects, is based on seeing but not on experiencing individual and singular particulars subsumed under the essences. For such judgments...individuals seen in phantasy, are sufficient. There is consciousness of what is seen, as sighted; it 'appears' but is not seized upon as factually existent. If, for example, we judge with eidetic universality, 'Any color whatever is different from any sound whatever,' the statement just made can be confirmed by examining our judging...Phantasy-intuition and eidetic intuition are there at the same time in a certain manner; but the latter intuition {the eidetic one} is not there as

one which makes the essence an object. It is, however, of the essence of the situation that we are at all times free to shift to the corresponding Objectivating attitude, and this shifting is precisely an essential potentiality. In accordance with the altered attitude, the judgment would be altered; it would then state 'The essence (the genus) color is other than the essence (the genus) sound.'[30]

Husserl is describing this subtle shift between seeing many examples of different colors in the mind's eye and diving into the essential differences of quality which lie at the bottom of their ultimate meaning, as grasped and unveiled in complete understanding. I can make a judgment of their differences based on the comparison of their mental images, while I am focused primarily on the images in imagination and secondarily focused on their eidetic constellations in the background. Or I can push away the mental images, and dive into the object-constellations of the genera themselves, as meaning-forms; (in both instances, one should remember that the sense of self or identity is attached to each mental image, and can also be created in the intuition of each genus).

Husserl wishes to contrast the ideal elements that appear while intuitively seeing the structures of consciousness (*noema, eidos*) along with their modalities of delivery (*noesis*) on the one hand, with the world that is perceived through external sense-impressions on the other. These irreal elements possess a virtual element to them in all the best

---

[30] Ideas I, p 13

Deleuzean sense. However, they still maintain a subjective residue, which Husserl did not see, but we might say that the region of this irreality was made up of certain remnants of the dying spiritual life as it is brought into the realm of thinking's activity in the subjective bubble. Their virtuality is dying down, but in the last moments of their death, they brighten up in consciousness one last time, with a certain intensity, like the final explosion of color in the autumn leaves. Nevertheless, when Husserl performs his epoché, he discovers that he has taken the world and its objects for granted. The projection of the representation that there is a 'real world of objects' out there is temporarily set aside. A new world is revealed through such an act – a world of meanings, pure acts of consciousness, and unitary ideal objects. This is an important move, even with its subjective limitations. Husserl describes it like this:

> By inquiring back into what was thus taken for granted...when we become conscious of it as 'presuppositions' and accord these their own universal and theoretical interest, then there opens up to us, to our growing astonishment, an infinity of ever new phenomena belonging to a new dimension, coming to light only through consistent penetration into the meaning- and validity-implications of what was thus taken for granted.[31]

---

[31] Husserl, Edmund. *The Crisis of European Sciences and Transcendental Phenomenology: An Introduction to Phenomenological Philosophy.* Trans. Carr. Northwestern UP, Evanston, Ill., 1970, pp. 111-112.

To focus on this new world of Intentionality for Brentano and Husserl is to be able to reflect on aspects of meaning that everyday language has difficulty expressing. For example, let us imagine that on a day in January, Luba is riding the train, and for a split second before the train disappears into a tunnel, she looks out the window and sees something unusual. After the train has disappeared into the darkness of the tunnel, she forms the idea (or the logical proposition) based on a perceptual judgment, 'It is snowing.' But unsure of her split-second judgment, Luba turns the glance of her ego toward the experience of a few moments earlier, and an image arises of light streaks and flakes of white floating through the air. Looking at the mental image brought up through remembering, Luba now forms the proposition in thought, 'It *is* snowing.' But when one attends to the intricate delivery of the meaning in this second context, one finds that it should be expressed, 'I, turning my reflective capacity toward a certain time, now perceive a mental image of a particular moment, where I clearly affirm that, based on the sense or meaning lying behind the mental image, it was indeed snowing at the time of the initial experience.' The first utterance, 'It is snowing' was dubiously received in the initial impression of the living now, so the assertion was held off until she could affirm it through memory. The meaning-nexus of the initial proposition ('it is snowing') is not equivalent to the second proposition. The first was a perceptual impression, giving rise to an initial formulation in the sense of a suspended perceptual judgment ('It seems that in this moment and position, precipitation is falling in the form of snow, but I am not entirely sure that this is a fact'). However, the second proposition is not only an experience of remembrance (rather than perception) giving rise to a mental image connected with its concept in thinking, but also an assertion or positive judgment regarding the fact that snow was falling. It should be noted, that Luba now possesses, in addition to the meaningful proposition, an affirmation of the actual existence of what it contains, something that was first pointed out by Brentano in *Psychology from an Empirical Standpoint.* In other words, she has made the judgment that the snow *actually exists* in this space and time.

Steiner, in his penetrating analysis of Brentano, reveals the spiritual reality that lies behind this affirmation of existence that takes place in such a judgment. He suggests that, no matter how long one may search, it is impossible to discover any direct physiological or psychological basis for the affirmation that an object actually exists in the relationship between the eyes and object. On the contrary, the determination that an object actually exists 'out there' is dependent on a third, indirect or mediating sense that colors or influences the intuition of an object: the sense of balance or equilibrium. The spirituality reality behind our normal sense of balance begins to be revealed only when we begin to cross the threshold. He describes that when a person attends to a particular object through one sense, it must be the case that at least one other sense operates simultaneously. The sense of equilibrium conveys information about our inner existence as it continually adjusts to the external world, and dimly impresses this changing relationship *in the form of a psychological (noetic) quality* added onto the perception or intuition. Steiner says:

> If there occurs the seeing of an object, for example, and at the same time our sense of balance is communicating an impression, what is seen will be sharply perceived. What is seen leads to a mental picture of the object. As a perception, our experience through the sense of balance remains dull; nevertheless, it manifests in the judgment that 'what I see exists' or 'that is what I see.'[32]

Steiner also reveals that there is a volitional or willful element inherent in every judgment of which Brentano remained unconscious. This is not just the turning of attention from one thought to another in the head. It is rather the fact that the human being is always woven into the will-life of the whole world warmth all around us. Brentano may have been too focused on his head to recognize the spiritual sense of balancing that was operating in the will both inside and outside the body. Steiner clarifies the basis for Brentano's notion of judgment by showing its direct connection to the body, soul, and spirit in different ways. He says the *spiritual* force of willing is dimly reflected in the metabolic activity of the physical body, and (as we have seen) in

---

[32] *Riddles of the Soul,* p 129. Also see pp 126-128 + 141-143 for the full complex and dense disclosure by Steiner.

affirmation or rejection of an object's existence in the *psychological sphere*. But the deeper spiritual force itself and most of its metabolic reflections remain unconscious to Brentano's descriptive psychology. The senses of balance and movement are involved because they are intimately woven with every perception. We can experience how the world seems to disappear when we are dizzy.[33] Indeed, it makes sense that an affirmation or rejection of the actuality of an object outside of the organism is related to the possibility of willfully interacting with such an object in movement. Such a volitional relationship with an actual object requires the continual adjustment of the self and the world, which is performed by the process of balancing and equilibration. Because I am a spirit woven together with the harmony and disharmony of the external world, and also a soul feeling itself with all the

---

[33] What Steiner says about this must be experienced directly to understand the issues at hand: "In a process of movement we also do not have to do physically with something whose essential being lies inside the organism, but rather with a working of the organism in relationships of balance and forces in which the organism is placed with respect to the outer world. Within the organism, the will is only assigned the role of a metabolic process; but the happening caused by this process is at the same time an actuality within the outer world's interrelation of balance and forces; and by being active in willing, the soul transcends the realm of the organism and participates with its deeds in the happenings of the outer world." *Riddles of the Soul,* p 139

rotations of the life of the earth and the cosmos, in order to inhabit and move a body and think about objects as external, and indeed, use them, I need to coordinate this vast living artistic machine. What a miracle that I am able to locate a screwdriver and use it with my hand! This coordination of the will, both within the mineral body and in the spiritual body woven together with the world, can unveil and explain the fundamental consciousness of an object or referent in all acts of meaning in the sphere of transcendental phenomenology. Indeed, we can even reverse the intensities in the relationship between seeing and balancing. When we cross the threshold and experience our spiritual wholeness, as it tries, moment by moment, to maintain its upright relationship to the central I-Am experience, rhythmically working in the folds of ether, soul, and spirit, we find that the amplitude of our sense of physical sight becomes diminished. In this case, we make the judgment in our consciousness, that it is the spiritual folds and weavings that actually exist, while the dead light of the physical world becomes dim. The awakening of the spiritual consciousness of the sense of equilibrium in movement only intensifies our sense of Self, but as a wholeness of thinking, feeling, and willing, pulsing round, under, out, and in. Steiner says, "Without a sense to convey this state of standing balanced, or of being poised, or of dancing in balance, we should be entirely unable to develop full consciousness."[34]

---

[34]*Man as a Being of Sense and Perception* (GA 206), lecture 1

Chapter 3 – The Dying Light: Intuition, Meaning-Fulfillment, and Noema

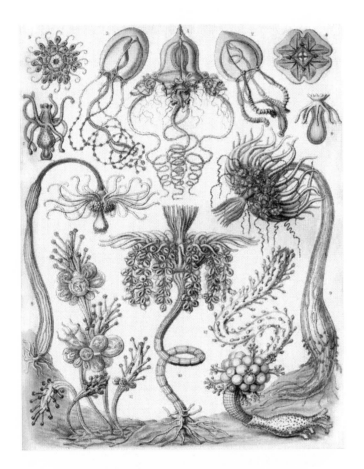

Tubulariae from Haeckel's *Artforms of Nature*

Let us continue with our careful elaboration of some of Husserl's ideas. In the *Logical Investigations*, Husserl introduced the important division between sensible and categorial intuition.[35] For example, Walter White may perceive the sensible features of a tomato by looking at it, smelling it and holding it in his hand. The red color, the malleable skin, and the acrid scent saturate his senses as soon as he turns his attention toward it. The senses then passively receive the perceptive features (*percepts*) of the various sides of the red object without any more activity on the part of the perceiver. This means that the empirical impressions are taken in directly through a *sensible intuition*. In full vividness, my eyes grasp the tiny curve and this bit of red. In this case, only what is sensed is registered, and there need not be any meaningful thought processes at all behind the bare

---

[35] Haddock and Hill describe categorial intuition very clearly: "Although we do not sensibly intuit anything that could correspond to the formal constituents of statements, there must be some act of intuition, similar to but different from that of sensible intuition, in which such 'formal' expressions are fulfilled. Husserl calls this sort of intuition, in which the meanings of the formal constituents are fulfilled and in which new categorically formed objectualities are constituted, categorial intuition...Categorial intuition neither glues together nor links sensible objects to produce a new sensible whole. If this were the case, the originally given in sensible intuition would be modified, and categorial intuition would be a falsifying reorganizing of the sensibly given. In such a case, the result would be a new sensible object." *Husserl or Frege*, pp 223-224

sense impressions. We must be clear, however, that the unity of the idea of tomato goes one step further than the pure moments of perceiving chaotic pieces and partial surfaces of redness as my eyes dart around.

To continue, Mr. White might also think over the issue further, "These three tomatoes are bigger than those three tomatoes." In this case, he is going beyond the sheer empirical data into the characteristically mental or noetic processes of collection (two groups of three tomatoes), comparison (A>B), and causality.[36] The connection and consolidation of the various angles of chaotic perception into one idea of tomato and its entire form (along with the backside of the object, which we never perceive simultaneously with the front) are also purely conceptual operations. One can perceive a single element of redness through sensible or empirical intuition, but when one begins to refer to whole objects, complete shapes, sets or relations, or more complex categories in individual propositions, one has entered into the realm of reflective, meaningful thought. Only reflective thought can determine types of *relationships* between empirical data; the passive empirical perception is powerless in this regard. This means that all scientific analysis of empirical data already must contain a conceptual element. It is sometimes hard for people to grasp that they do not perceive groups of objects, but only perceive

---

[36]Robert Sokolowski accurately outlines this in his beautifully written book, *Husserlian Meditations*, Northwestern UP, Evanston, Ill., 1974, pp. 30-42.

disconnected fragments, and can only unite percepts into wholes and groups through thinking. You never perceive all of the objects in Picasso's "Guernica" as a whole, you only group them into a whole through thinking's synthetic and set-forming activity. The dream of a purely self-determining positivistic science is impossible. A human must always unite the chaotic momentary sense impressions into ideas of wholeness, identities, sets, consistency, and relationships, using thinking. Certainly, some scientists don't really perceive their thinking as another realm of reality, and of course, our normal construction of the mental representation as a unity of the percepts and the concepts takes place at lightning speed and mostly happens passively and unconsciously, but this does not change the inner reality.

More than this, when Mr. White realizes for the first time that tomato group A is bigger than tomato group B because of the conditions of light in the garden, his understanding becomes saturated with the meaning of these connections and relations. The man is no longer focusing his attention on the merely sensible qualities of the individual tomato, but rather is 'glancing the ray of his ego' toward a set of tomatoes and its causal connections; in other words, in some degree of consciousness, he is 'intending a categorial object.' Husserl calls this categorial or *pure intuition.*[37] Categorial intuitions are oriented toward

---

[37] *Ideas I* pp 78-79. He says here that axioms are not expressive of facts of empirical experience, but developed

the sphere of acts of meaning, rather than toward the data of empirical perception. It has to do with 'categories' since these are larger 'groups' or features or prototypes that are never outwardly seen. We never see an 'animal' in general, we only see one side of a specific duck, mongoose, or crab. We only think the concept or category of animal with our barely conscious powers of grasping ideas. Intuiting sense features is like using a tube that only sucks in color and sound stuff; intuiting ideas is like another tube that only sucks in meaning stuff. Notice carefully how you can move from the use of one 'tube' to the other 'tube.' This rough simile is only used to give another means of clarifying the difference between external perception and watching thinking as it happens.

The interesting thing about humans referring to categorial features in thought is that they may 'see' them on a continuum from full vivid saturation in intuition to an empty representation through inner words or linguistic association of meaning. Some people mistakenly believe that the signs they use in their mental process exhaust the full nature of thinking. Not by a long shot! The fundamental disagreement between 'continental' and 'analytical' philosophy is based on this one misunderstanding, among others. Empty or unsaturated representation or formal reference is like hearing the TV in the living room while standing in the kitchen. I can't see the screen. In this case, I can only describe the appearance

---

expressions of data from eidetic intuition, given in fullness of insight.

of the pots, counters, and spatulas in the kitchen while only referring at a distance to what is happening in the living room. Seeing mental images as images is like watching the TV while you are in the same room. With eidetic cognition, I am also watching the TV in the same room, but it is now as if the images on the screen are partially ignored, and I am seeing a second TV screen behind the first one, which is full of pure meaning forms, categories and ideas. Goethe's level of imagination arises, when the real events filmed on the screens flow together with the observer's soul, and arise as a new and complete image. Full spiritual perception only arrives, then, when one is able to look at oneself objectively from the outside, and with morality and the gift of the grace of the otherness arising from the real events and the TVs, one merges with both of the televisions, while remaining conscious. In this moment, one flows into the TVs and all events and rooms, and sees that the various televisions and material rooms are illusions and that there are only spiritual beings and planes that exist, interpenetrating one another. So much for this analogy.

Even people who are legitimately bumping up against spiritual reality do not always see ideas or memories in a fully imagistic way. Soul and spiritual reality can first appear more in a way of touching and being touched, for example. Schiller had a highly developed sense for art, but yet only saw individual plants with his eyes, and only used strings of words inside his head to refer to sense objects. He was thinking in concepts, but could not see his concepts.

Goethe could look at individual plants with his eyes, and could also see the archetypal plant in full saturation in his life body where imaginations show up. This is why most human conversations are simply an exchange of memorized opinions, and why we do not always attend to the expression of meaning itself as we talk. Our intuition is not fully saturated in its acquisition of conceptual content, moment by moment. This often leads us to miss the depth of what is being expressed in the other person's words. No wonder we don't get along!

Husserl was able to clarify some of these intricate processes with incredible detail in his phenomenological works. Let us consider some examples. Later on in the day, Luba might report to her mother in a hasty and breathless monologue the fact that it was snowing earlier as she rode the train. As she utters the words, 'It was snowing,' she merely emptily refers to (or *intends*) the primary perceptual impression, which was stored and is now accessible through remembrance. She does not gaze in a concentrated manner into her process of memory, nor does she once again analyze the memory image before her mind's eye. The words serve to signify the meaning of the statement, but in a manner that is quite 'distant' and 'vague.' She barely considers the concept of snow at all and it is only dimly contained in the course of her conversation. She is watching her mother's face the whole time.

On another day, suppose that Gwen Stacy is watching the snow fall, and she reaches out her hand

and catches three snowflakes, putting them quickly under a microscope set up outside. She discovers for the first time that they are beautiful hexagonal shapes made of ice crystals, and she then closes her eyes and focuses on the new aspects she has been able to add to her concept of snow. She concentrates on the meaning of snow, letting her former presuppositions and images fall out of play. She understands the meaning of snow in a completely new manner, and her categorial intuition of the concept of snow with all of its connections is fully intended. Before when she had thought or spoken about snow, it had a meaning feature that was much vaguer and more incomplete, but now the meaning of snow has become completely filled in and registered. The essence of the concept of snow is revealed. Husserl calls this procedure of moving from an empty or confused meaning-intention to a fulfilled intention, 'identity synthesis.'[38]

---

[38] *Logical Investigations*, Part VI, (§ 8). He says, "From the tranquil, as it were *static* coincidence of meaning and intuition, we now turn to that *dynamic* coincidence where an expression first functions in merely symbolic fashion, and then is accompanied by a 'more or less' corresponding intuition. Where this happens, we experience a descriptively peculiar consciousness of fulfilment: the act of pure meaning, like a goal-seeking intention, finds its fulfilment in the act which renders the matter intuitive. In this transitional experience, the mutual belongingness of the two acts, the acts of meaning, on the one hand, and the intuition which more or less corresponds to it, reveals its phenomenological roots. We experience how the same objective item which was 'merely thought of' in symbol is now presented in intuition, and that it is intuited as being precisely the determinate so-and-so that it was a first merely thought or meant to be. We are merely expressing

The 'empty meaning intention' or reference is like hearing the dialogue and music from <u>Mad Men</u> on the TV while I am standing in the kitchen. At first, I can hear Don, Roger, and Peggy's voices, but I do not see the actions in full color. I can even tell my wife in the kitchen a little bit about who is speaking and what is happening in a general way. Meaning fulfillment is like walking into the living room from the kitchen, and now being able to see precisely what is happening, and also finding the second category-TV screen that shows up behind the first. I begin to see not only Don and Roger laughing on the primary screen, but I can also dive into the concepts of secretary, typewriter, whisky, scarf, advertising, and so on projected on the second TV screen 'behind' the first.

---

the same fact if we say that the intentional essence of the act of intuition gets more or less perfectly fitted into the semantic essence of the act of expression. In the previously considered static relation among acts of meaning and intuition, we spoke of a recognition, a knowing...But the element of meaning is not here itself the act of recognition. In the purely symbolic understanding of a word, an act of meaning is performed (the word means something to us) but nothing is thereby known, recognized. The difference lies...not in the mere accompanying presence of the intuition of the thing named, but in the phenomenological peculiar form of unity. What is characteristic about this unity of knowing, or recognition, is now shown up by the dynamic relationship before us. In it there is at first the meaning-intention, quite on its own: then the corresponding intuition comes to join it. At the same time, we have the phenomenological unity which is now stamped as a consciousness of fulfilment."

Compare this to a third example of Gwen Stacy standing on a bridge, watching the snow falling down on a lazy afternoon, thinking to herself, 'It is snowing.' In this instance, her sensuous intuition is fully saturated, but what is signified by her string of representations (or propositions) is a combination of the primary impression that she is receiving from her environment in the living now, and the concept of snow, determined as actually existent through her sense of equilibrium. In this case there is a dual operation taking place, consisting of a complete registration of the percepts through the sensible intuition, and a corresponding meaning-component referring to the concept of snow and existence. As is common in such situations, she is probably only hazily aware of the complete nature of the concept of snow as an ideal object in pure intuition, while her senses, and her intentions, are more or less completely engrossed in the primary perceptual impression of the snow. Categorial and sensible intuitions can be oriented toward a single object in two different epistemological apprehensions simultaneously, but one is more conscious than the other. Brentano himself was also quite adamant in pointing out the difference between the process of perception and the mental-object perceived in situations like this, and Steiner confirmed the difficulty many people have in becoming conscious of it:

> Actually, this "failure to recognize the most obvious differences" {as Brentano said} is no rare occurrence. It is based on the fact that our power of mental picturing can unfold the necessary

attentiveness only for sense impressions, whereas the actual soul activity that is also occurring is present to consciousness as little as what is experienced in a state of sleep. We are dealing here with two streams of experience; one of these is apprehended in a waking state; the other – the soul stream – is grasped simultaneously, but only with an attentiveness as weak as the mental perception we have in sleep, i.e., it is hardly grasped at all.[39]

Husserl calls the content of this 'soul activity,' which is the changing element in the dynamic process of the identity synthesis, and oriented toward the *specifically intended meaning* at a point in time, the 'noema.'[40] The noemata are the various senses,

---

[39] Brentano discusses it in *Research into a Psychology of the Senses* (1907) quoted in Steiner, *Riddles of the Soul,* pp 10-12. To strengthen this inner awareness, one could follow Steiner's indications in *Knowledge of the Higher Worlds*, chapters 1 and 2.

[40] See Husserl, *Ideas I*, pghs 88-133. A noema has three features or branches: 1) a limb reaching toward the objective meaning, 2) an inherent quality that can be imagistic, resonant, or force-like, and 3) a limb dipping in the undercurrent of its manner of presentation (thetic quality) demonstrating in which mode (remembrance, perception, etc) it came to consciousness. Husserl uses the term *vergegenwärtigen* [to visualize, make an impression, bring to mind or awareness] to indicate the appearance of the fluctuating light or image qualities of the noema which are perceived livingly in the mind's eye. This term is unfortunately often translated as 'presentation.' The resonant or force-like quality of consciousness that Husserl recognizes in the noema (but only in a vague manner) is, in its deeper, spiritual scientific sense, a condensation of a

possible forms, and explicit associations of idea elements as they are seen and experienced in the soul's eye. When the image features of the current noemata are varied, they can be purified to become the eidos proper. When this is the case, a higher region appears, where the meaning structure itself takes shape in the flexible fabric of the fluid of pure potentiality or virtuality. But during any conscious intuition of these mental images, one can note how these specific noemata are oriented and sucked together into one background concept, which is the noematic core. When the noematic core is recognized in its underlying identity as an objectivity, and when it is clearly seen in the eyes of intuition, it becomes the twisting and turning, self-transforming eidos, an eidetic virtuality. Let us consider the noema in more detail.

---

particular kind of light in the soul. There is no doubt that, from Steiner's perspective, the noema functions at the level of personal idea or representation (*Vorstellung*). This is part of his point in his comment about Husserl's viewpoint on the Cologne cathedral. One can, of course, look at the whole structure of the noema from the soul and spiritual side, to recognize the particular layers of soul and etheric light that undergird what Husserl calls the noema. One should also note that the term 'intendings' is often used to translate *Vorstellungen* in Husserl. As Steiner shows in *The Philosophy of Freedom*, the *Vorstellung* is indeed a 'personalized concept,' however, the faculties of the spiritual researcher operate outside this bubble of personal intentions.

For example, when a luthier considers different ways of changing the tonal quality on a cello design, he or she may focus on various components of the instrument: first considering the bridge (the piece of wood supporting the strings on the face of the body), then the neck, then the type of wood, etc. When he or she is sitting mulling over these features without actually handling a particular instrument and looking it over, the aspects of the cello are variously intuited as categorial components having a different conceptual interior. Let us imagine that as the designer hones in on the bridge design - first she focuses on the *shape* of the wood as a theme. The particular and nuanced sense or meaning (*Sinn*) of the bridge that the luthier accesses in the mind's eye at a specific time possesses a conceptual character that differs from the conceptual character of a consideration of the bridge in terms of its *placement* on the cello's carved top. Furthermore, the quality of the act of thinking of these elements and holding various mental images or memories in the mind's eye, changes from moment to moment. This 'actual soul quality' that Steiner describes in the quote above, can be brought to clearer consciousness. Not only the meaning-structure itself, but also the warmth, feeling, and will forces that operate 'behind the scenes' in order to allow a person to think about one idea, mental image, or another. What 'arms' allow you to rotate a memory image, for example? Why do you move your eyes when you are searching for a concept? Both categorial intuitions are filled with the meaning or concept of a 'bridge,' but in two different presentations, representations, or mental pictures (and each act of being conscious of the specific nuance also has its own resonance or quality-sensation). The noema is, one might say, halfway between a specific mental image with its one vantage point, and a concept, with its absence of pictorial content.

Husserl describes the noematic aspect drawn from what is grasped in outer perception, "the tree simpliciter can burn up, be resolved into its chemical elements, etc. But the sense – the meaning of this perception, something belonging necessarily to its essence – cannot burn up; it has no chemical elements, no forces, no real properties. Everything which is purely immanent and reduced in the way peculiar to the mental process, everything which cannot be conceived apart from it just as it is in itself, and which *eo ipso* passes over into the Eidos in the eidetic attitude, is separated by an abyss from all of Nature and physics and no less from all psychology – and even this image, as naturalistic, is not strong enough to indicate the difference."[41]

He is correct that the essential realm which appears in intuition on the concept plane does not immediately show its connection with the world perceived in the natural attitude. The realm of meaning, whether subjective or objective, seems to be separated from the world as understood by the natural sciences. Nevertheless, Husserl cannot see the second abyss that must be crossed in order to be able to see these elements in the true sphere of concepts, which

[41] *Ideas I*, pgh 89

are indeed spiritual beings, that one first becomes conscious of, when the inner light begins to shine in the astral body.[42] True, what he sees in the eidos is **connected to** the soul and spiritual worlds, but his viewing of them lies in the consciousness soul, on the subjective side of the threshold.

The noema is not just made of the particular mental images or light formations that fluctuate in imagination, as one visualizes various ways to support the strings on a viol. It is also immediately connected with the sense or meaning of what is considered, and it remains rooted in the strata from which it came. Just like you must think to understand the actions of the baseball teams in front of your eyes at a game, you must also think to understand the raw images you may see in your mind's eye. The image of a red door could be seen in the mind's eye without any understanding, which means with no eidetic or conceptual element bringing unity, understanding, and wholeness from 'behind.' The noematic core appears, when I can turn the mental image in any direction, but it always remains a door. I stand within the substance and light of the meaning of any door with my thinking, feeling, and willing Self.

Furthermore, Husserl says that when you are intuiting the noema, you always remember if you are operating in the flow of the present, in anticipation, or in memory, for example. After performing 'the eidetic

---

[42] See Steiner's *Initiation and the Passing Moment,* lecture 4

reduction' with imaginative variation (which we will discuss more in the next chapter), the noema as a whole can receive a new creative influx of meaning. From the sphere of spiritual science, we would say that the concept is expanded or opened. As you approach the transition zone between what is subjective and what is objective, it can also happen that you begin to visualize the inner light streams swimming on a giant 'game board.' One can rise up to perceive a thousand new elements on a giant board or screen of infinite riddles. This also must be 'read' or interpreted to have meaning. Husserl never goes so far as to describe this first grid per se, but he begins to see its elements in a vague and schematic manner. This first grid is not yet the objective spiritual world, but is the geometrical visual plane onto which the dying etheric life is injected from the cosmos. It becomes conscious in the intellectual-soul experience as mental images. The will elements of thinking activity become conscious in the consciousness soul's activity. This head-centered vision can also lead into subjective illusion, as is the case with visionary experiences coming from drugs or the first attempts at meditation, before one approaches the true guardian of the threshold. Its luciferic tendency must be overcome by a new Christ-centered morality and devotion in the heart.[43] We will discuss this issue throughout.

---

[43] The luciferic tends toward an enclosed, subjective and personal ecstasy, while the Christ element leads toward an earthly-cosmic experience of a freely creative I-AM that has learned how to join the individual with the center of all humanity through the heart. We will discuss this in more

Nevertheless, Husserl is correct that this imaginative variation of all possible cello bridges, opens up new ideas that were never approached before. The understanding receives new concepts, configurations, and inspirations. It is an effective process of researching a topic at the level of normal consciousness. But Husserl also experiences what he calls 'remarkable changes in consciousness' when he views the essences in their 'own peculiar dimension.' [44] These statements are ignored by those philosophers who want to interpret Husserl more in the vein of linguistic analysis and formal logic, from the 'analytic side.' One does not have to transform consciousness to start to think about logic in an abstract sense! So where does this change in consciousness come from?

The awareness that rises in moments of consciousness, whether sensible or in the

---

detail below. One knows and perceives that one is a free individuality in the moment that one can simultaneously create concepts, and perceive or intuit the I who is creating the thoughts. This is just as possible as it is for me to breathe in oxygen and breathe out carbon dioxide. I am an individual being who can nonetheless engage in many different things at the same time. Only people who have not experienced this essence of thinking say that it is not possible. It is Lucifer and Ahriman speaking in such denials. The luciferic and ahrimanic doubles cannot create your concepts while you are conscious of producing them as a free thinker in moral intuition. They can only steal the energy of concepts and representations that you adopt unconsciously in running through thought-images. They think you, but you believe you are a free personality. This is why 'confront while experience' is necessary as a spiritual foundation.

[44] *Ideas I*, pgh 92

understanding, is produced by the invisible forces of death operating in the etheric world. The elevation to a new level of consciousness in the sphere of categories that Husserl experienced was produced by an intensification of the normal imaginative faculties. This produces an accumulation of the supersensible substance that is dying. But it also, paradoxically, can pull in new ideas that are also dimming down and become paralyzed structures in and around the head. We see that if one does not cross the threshold into the spiritual world, the penetration to the level of the noema and the subsequent attempts at subjective imaginative variation, can actually produce a larger barrier to access this spiritual world. From a spiritual scientific point of view, subjective eidetic research and imaginative variation can actually nourish Lucifer and Ahriman even more. This does not mean that we should not attempt it, but it can only become valuable when we begin to cross the threshold through thinking in the precise sense of the intuitive thinking from *The Philosophy of Freedom*. When we view the process from the spiritual side, we can now recognize that if the strictly controlled will forces and imaginative elements that are poured into the concrete imaginative variation are erased, released, and grasped with devotion in the heart, then this can allow the spiritual beings to pour down new elements of themselves into the human understanding. I also pour some of my self out to meet them. One must hold on to the real I AM who thinks and moves concepts. The fields and mountains of thought-space are expanded, and new ideas are received as inspiration. One could imagine a new kind of cello or bass bridge built of a magnetic field which repels the strings, or one that isolates each string and has a rounded eye through which the string passes, but supported from above rather than underneath, for example. But Husserl only perceived this whole process of new meaning revelation up to certain limits. The Spirits of Motion elevate the previous work of the Spirits of Form, and the human being, who is always standing in the midst of their godly work, receives new nourishment in thought, which he then condenses, paralyzes and stores inside his subjective bubble as a particular mental image, word, or linkages of ideas.[45] She weaves her personal self in this way, and that is perfectly acceptable. The spiritual researcher, can now learn how to leave some of the living element of the inspiration alive on the other side of the threshold, using morality, love, and devotion, where she is still connected in consciousness with the spiritual parts of her being. We can then experience the pain of how the world dies in each representation. This skill is described with great intimacy and precision in Ben-Aharon's *The Event in Science, History, Philosophy & Art,* chapter 3.

When one perceives a cello with a fully saturated sensible intuition, two aspects are united in one process of understanding: the percepts (with their material conditions or *hyle*) and the specific idea-form (*noema*). Husserl always seems to think that the percepts themselves, the bare colors and sensations, always have a meaning aspect associated with them (the 'explicative characteristics'). It is because he was

---

[45] See Steiner, GA 266b, p 192

not able to separate the pure qualities of sensation, affect, and perception from the pure conceptual activity of thinking. But he is not alone in this failure. People like Merleau-Ponty and Deleuze go further in this regard of purifying and analyzing the pure percept-flow. The furthest aspect of this procedure can lead one into the etheric world itself, as described in Steiner's work, and expanded by Ben-Aharon in *Cognitive Yoga* (which concentrates especially on spiritualizing the process of sensation and perception). Through this spiritualization of perception, one can return to and resurrect the new vision of mother nature. This is another little key to find the Mothers.

This is difficult to understand and must be directly lived through in the moral etherization of perception. In truth, the bare percepts in ordinary consciousness have no meaning in themselves. The spirits of color, for example, are totally killed, ignored, and reversed in everyday conscious perception of what is incorrectly called 'color'. The only residue is in the dead outer glow of the play of shadow and brightness in the non-moral physical 'light' that shines on landscapes. In addition, in normal consciousness, the dead outer glow of physical 'color' is rudely linked up with a personal concept on the mental representation plane which gives the external form and color its only earthly 'meaning.' We must remember and experience the moral element that is at stake when Steiner says, "The perception therefore is not something finished, not something self-contained, but one side of the total reality. The other side is the concept. The act of knowledge is the synthesis of perception and concept."[46]

Let us now turn our attention to the modes of approach and the activity of moving the rays of attention. The noematic core is, as we have seen, the relative goal of meaning fulfillment. On the other hand, the *process* or act of changing thematic focus or altering the mode of conceptual engagement from (e.g.) belief to imagination, or to memory, or to focusing on the analysis of parts is called by Husserl the *noesis*. *The noesis is like the mode and direction of access and the noema is the specific nuance of meaningful content in the act.* It is obvious that the process of opening up different regions of conscious focus has an element of will in it, which Husserl could barely penetrate with consciousness. I also must remember that I possess a 'region of beliefs' and a 'region of memory' in order to open up the doorway into the specific noetic mode each time. I know how to access the realm of imagination in contrast to the realm of memory, and my will can open its doors. For it is the will that moves the 'rays' of attention from

---

[46] GA 4, <p 92>. Steiner also indicates the moral quality of colors vs. the dying outer image in a variety of places. Also - "This activity of thinking is one filled with content. For it is only through a quite definite, concrete content that I can know why the snail belongs to a lower level of organization than the lion. The mere sight, the perception, gives me no content which can inform me about the degree of perfection of an organization." Nevertheless, new concepts can arise when perception is spiritualized once again.

one 'room', concept or position to another, whether in perception or in thinking. Can you find the cold fingers that do this? Can you find the warm clouds that accomplish this? It is a fine game of hide and seek.

For Husserl, the noetic activity that is oriented toward the noematic core, means that when the mechanic considers different features of the automotive transmission, which present different noemata in the sphere of representations, as he moves from one theme to another, he nevertheless maintains a continual reference toward the meaning of 'transmission' as a unitary concept. Husserl says, "The glancing ray of the pure Ego, parting into a plurality of rays, rests in the act of fulfillment upon the X that is coming to synthetic unity."[47] This X is the fundamental meaning of any logical proposition. Regarding the will aspect of moving observation from one place to another, Husserl says, "The ray of attention presents itself as emanating from the pure Ego and terminating in that which is objective, as directed to it or being diverted from it. The ray does not become detached from the Ego; on the contrary, it is itself an Ego-ray, and remains an Ego-ray. The 'Object' is struck; it is the target; it is put into a relation to the Ego (and by the Ego itself) but it is not 'subjective.'"[48]

---

[47] *Ideas I*, pgh 131. See pages <192-193>
[48] Ibid, p <192>..

In one sense, Husserl shows just how deeply he has penetrated and seen the structural elements of the will that function in the normal process of representing in the area in and around the head. The 'rays' can actually be seen as they work like many tentacles in the realm of intentionality. This requires an inner perception that neither Kant nor Hegel possessed. However, the spiritual researcher goes further. Through careful development, we pass beyond the personal, while maintaining a link with everyday consciousness. It eventually becomes intimately clear as the situation is more expansively and precisely seen from the spiritual scientific side, that these rays of the ego which Husserl describes are totally subjective. In this he is completely mistaken because he could not see himself from outside of his personal etheric boundaries and his personal soul envelopes. The spiritual I who really thinks outside the notion of subjective or objective, and beyond the idea of inside or outside the body, does not direct the process from a secure tower inside the head of the personal body. It is only after entering the spiritual world that one sees how the will of the higher spiritual self directs its activity in relationship to a whole community of beings. Only one who has experienced 'It Thinks me' can relate to the difference between the Ahrimanic will-tentacles in the personal soul body, the personal desires of the Lucifer double, and the higher spiritual forces of will working in spiritualized thinking proper. Eventually, the higher and lower wills are integrated through spiritual scientific work focused in the heart, as one can read in Steiner and Ben-Aharon. Nevertheless, to describe the actual relationship between the spiritual will and the rays of the subjective will is extremely difficult and one of the ongoing riddles to solve in coordinating the higher self and the lower self in spiritual scientific practice. This is a lot of fun, and each individual must do it for himself.

From another angle, much of the work of the French post-structuralists was focused on showing that what Husserl thought was 'objective' still maintained a great deal of subjective residue and a wide variety of unconscious presuppositions. The personal ego in its imaginary panopticon does not really control all of the meaning in its world. Deleuze in particular exposed and dug beyond many limits in Husserl's project. Here is one important example:

> [Husserl claims that] in this nucleus of noematic sense, there appears something even more intimate, a 'supremely' or transcendentally intimate 'center,' which is nothing other than the relation between sense [or meaning] itself and the object in its reality...At the heart of the logic of sense [or meaning], one always returns to this problem, this immaculate conception, being the passage from sterility to genesis. But the Husserlian genesis seems to be a slight-of-hand...the relation between sense [or meaning] and object is the natural result of the relation between noematic predicates – a something = x, which is capable of functioning as their support or principle of unification. This thing = x is not at all therefore like a nonsense internal and co-present to sense, or a zero-point presupposing nothing of

what it necessarily engenders. It is rather the Kantian object = x, where x means 'in general.' It has in relation to sense an extrinsic, rational relation of transcendence, and gives itself, ready-made, the form of denotation, just as meaning, as a predicable generality, was giving itself, ready-made, the form of signification. It seems that Husserl does not think about genesis on the basis of a necessarily 'paradoxical' instance, which properly speaking, would be 'non-identifiable (lacking its own identity and its own origin). He thinks of it, on the contrary, on the basis of an originary faculty of common sense...in the position of a transcendental subject, which retains the form of the person, of personal consciousness, and of subjective identity, and which is satisfied with creating the transcendental out of the characteristics of the empirical...In fact, this bestowal of meaning, on the basis of the immanent quasi-cause...may occur only within a transcendental field which would correspond to the conditions posed by Sartre in his decisive article of 1937: an impersonal transcendental field, not having the form of a synthetic personal consciousness or a subjective identity – with the subject, on the contrary, being always constituted.[49]

Deleuze's critique is extremely valuable, as I have shown in my other writings. The zero point and the impersonal shock of the moral concept-planes beyond the first noematic field (the provisional head-centered concept plateau) are the places where one must

---

[49] *The Logic of Sense*, pp 97-99

journey to meet the further transformations arriving at the threshold to the spiritual world. Deleuze shows us precisely what it takes to escape from the labyrinth of the false image of subjective representation and ego-driven coordination of meaning. It can be a scary and confusing place. Indeed, spiritual scientific development and research must go even further in elaborating and experiencing the differences between the real I awakening in Spiritual Imaginative Cognition, the fractured personae on the Deleuzean planes, and the ego in transcendental phenomenology. To experience the differences in reality means to change one's entire soul and being. But let us now continue by considering one of the closest links between Goethe, Husserl and Steiner. This concerns the development of 'eidetic variation.'

Chapter 4 – Is the World Imagining Me?
The Riddle of Imaginative Variation

Discomedusae from Haeckel's *Artforms of Nature*

Husserl is able to reach toward his refined sense of an idealism, which is grounded securely enough in self-evidence to provide a legitimate foundation for any possible science, by means of a specific methodology that reveals the archetypal or essential forms of the ideal objects pertinent to these sciences. This method takes place in the sphere of the phenomenological reduction, in the realm of imagination, and begins by turning the categorial intuition toward noematic-pictorial instances of relevant types of objects. For example, one could imagine a large number of different mammals, in clear and focused mental pictures, and in a playful but concentrated manner begin to alter the properties of these images in any way one chooses. We might transform the clearly lit-up image of a rabbit into an elephant by expanding the shape, size, coloring, and every other quality of the rabbit until the elephant is in intuitive view as a steadfast image.[50] We then

---

[50] Husserl continuously strives to grasp the mental structures and the images that appear in the sphere of intentionality with more and more clarity. He says, "That which floats before us in fluid unclarity, with a greater or less intuitional remoteness, must therefore be brought into normal nearness and made perfectly clear before it can be used as the basis for a correspondingly valuable eidetic intuition in which the essences and the eidetic relationships intended to attain perfect givenness. Thus, the seizing upon essences itself has its degrees of clarity, as does the single

continue moving through a wide variety of other examples until a particular type of categorial object or conceptual framework comes into view in a higher sphere, which consists of the boundary conditions, essential determinations, and the fundamental productive notion at the bottom of every possible mammal. Because we are operating without the presuppositions of positivistic natural science, and are no longer concerned with cases of external fact as actually existent, we are permitted to stretch the fantasy as far as it takes us, while researching all of the possible species that could exist. We could imagine the *Discomedusae* that Haeckel illustrates from infinite angles, sizes, and profiles. We might therefore imagine some chimerical creature that does not exist, possessing the features of a sea-creature, mouse, lion, and mammoth combined. This fluidity of thought, which takes serious effort and many years to properly cultivate, then reveals the eidos. The particular images

---

particular floating before us. However, just as there is for the moment corresponding to it in the individual, there is for any essence an absolute nearness, so to speak, in which its givenness, compared to the series of degrees of clarity, in an absolute – i.e., a pure givenness of it itself." <126> *Ideas I.* And also…"Insofar as a residue of unclarity remains, it casts a shadow over certain moments in that which is 'itself' given, and accordingly, those moments remain outside the circle of light suffusing the purely given." <136> *Ideas I.* But this "clarity" of Husserl's contains moral, epistemological, and spiritual-scientific problems as has been shown by Derrida, Deleuze, Ben-Aharon, and others. One must find the living supersensible streams of warmth that flow below and around the central crystallization of representations in the dying light ether.

are set aside, and another self-evolving fabric of flexibility appears, which is connected to the region of thinking, and thoroughly penetrated with meaning. Husserl's descriptions of this inner region of concept forms, which are fluid but perfectly clear, vivid, and completely near and saturated, always refer to their uniqueness. He is standing in them with the immediate understanding of their morphology, connections, significations, and boundaries, but they are like nothing seen in the sense world. He says that the images used as a basis for imaginative or eidetic variation:

> ...present their essence to us; the individual intuition turns itself around, which itself is an eidetic possibility, into eidetic intuition, or into the attitude of thinking which on the ground of intuition grasps eidetic states of affairs in pure concepts and expresses them.[51]

---

[51] Husserl, Edmund. *Ideas III,* Hague, 1980 p 35. There is a whole tradition of work in projective geometry (arising from Steiner's inspiration) which can be effectively linked to Husserlian imaginative variation. Likewise, the wonderful thought-experiments of Bucky Fuller (such as the realization that multiple inner and outer triangles are created when the boundaries of a single triangle are drawn), also take place, more or less, in the same region where Husserl's imaginative variation took place. Of course, Husserl penetrated further into the minute elements of the consciousness soul and its logical and mental structures than almost anyone at any time in history. But at the same time, the capacity to access the realm of imaginative variation by whatever means should not be confused with fully fledged Spiritual Imagination in Steiner's sense.

In an analogous way to the manner in which the noematic nucleus provides a synthetic identity to the concrete instances of meaning-intentions concerning a single theme or object, the eidos is an essential ideal form that governs any possible manifestation of particular instances. One could say that the rule governing the elements of a set contains describable features that are not found in any of the elements of the set. The wholeness of the mother is only found virtually in every actual part. Furthermore, the mother can be seen with the objective Imagination faculty, or with scientific extrasensory perception. The creative power of the 'empty category' is the producer of its offspring, it is not the mere container in which they are gathered afterwards. In the same way, the prototypical plant-idea in Goethe shows directly, as it is intuited, that it can produce any plant from itself infinitely. For Husserl, the eidos or essence

---

Unfortunately, these two totally different regions and experiences are almost universally lumped together by people who have not yet experienced true Imagination. This happens when people read but do not devotedly penetrate into the spiritual and soul life of Anthroposophy in real experience. It is also the case, by the way, that the perceptual afterimage cannot give us, by itself, access to the spiritual world, despite the wishes of many people that it could. The afterimage does not overcome the basic orientations formed by Lucifer and Ahriman in us. Until the reversal is seen for what it is, the afterimage is no help. Such people wish for the entry to the spiritual world to be easily understood, and easily achieved, without real self-transformation and the difficult process of an Anthroposophical spiritualization of thinking.

(*Wesen*) then can provide a universal basis for an ontological stratification that permits the determinate objects researched by the various scientific disciplines to be hierarchically arranged by category and region. For example, we discover that the intuition (whether sensible or categorial) of individual animals always contains an essential feature that clearly separates these intuitions from those of plants. This imaginative process should not be confused with the outcome of a hallucinatory fantasy. Husserl is convinced that free variation, used as a rigorous scientific methodology, can reveal the necessary foundations of any discipline. The eidetic essences reveal themselves as identical through different times and demonstrate themselves as impossible of being otherwise.[52]

At the ground of every material science must then be the self-giving of the possible boundary forms of objective research, what Husserl calls an 'a priori science.' The eide are the necessary and archetypal forms of possible objects that are referred to in specific

---

[52] Hill & Haddock define his technique this way: "By means of the comparative variation of the founding sensible acts and its corresponding referents, we become conscious of the identity of the species as the general object of which the objects of the plurality of possible founding acts are mere instantiations." *Husserl or Frege?* p 226. You can follow Husserl's gradual discovery of the usefulness of imaginative variation in his notes and journals which are now being published, for example, pp 30-32 in *Zur Lehre Vom Wesen und zur Methode der Eidetischen Variation (Texte aus dem Nachlass, 1891 – 1935),* Springer 2012. Bolzano also used a method of 'propositional variation' earlier in the 19th century.

judgments and propositions, but these eidetic objects "possess after all a pure essence fixable prior to all judicative content."[53] One can understand, then that in terms of intentional objects discovered in phenomenology, these eidetic essences are the highest stage and final goal of meaning fulfillment in Husserl's transcendental project. Of course, a precise scientific language will be necessary to communicate the eidetic features, but language can no more fully express the eidos, than a whole book could completely describe the minute details of the flowers, grasses, birds, and colors in a single overgrown field. Linguistic formulations and structures are necessarily grounded in the pre-linguistic noemata and eide that populate the sphere of meaning, and Husserl suggests that there is a natural connection between the linguistic expression and the essences themselves.[54] We find the deeper cause of this if we step into the realm of spiritual science, where we discover that there is an inner word that flows through all unfolding life at all moments.

However, it must be made absolutely plain that the eidetic essences are not abstract linguistic definitions that are discovered through a critical reflection (in the sense of the Kantian transcendental deduction) about what features would be essential and inessential to a particular concept or activity. The noema is not a metaphor for Husserl. But the cave of Plato was also not a metaphor. True, Husserl does not

---

[53] *Ideas III*, p 25
[54] *Ideas III*, pp 22 – 30

yet see the sun outside the cave, but he begins to get close to the exit of the cave. Discovering the eidos is not a reverse deductive process taking place while one maintains the natural attitude of the positivistic sciences, and concentrates on the perceptible features of the external world, rather it is a direct experience of a lit-up object, an individual entity, in a noematic field that is arranged much like a visual field. The ray of categorial intuition is unified with an individual object in its terrain that presents itself from the 'front' or horizon, and although it is not an individual image, it is the malleable source for possible images.[55] Cognizing the essences is "the acquisition of a new region of being never before delineated in its own peculiarity – a region which, like any other genuine region, is a region of individual being."[56] It is experienced in a full saturation of categorial intuition, analogous in its degree of saturation to watching a movie with the external senses. To be even more precise, it is essential to differentiate at this point between three regions and manners of presentation in the mind's eye, where a mental image can come to consciousness with the eyes closed.

---

[55] Eventually, one can uncover supersensible features of meaning and image from all sides of the body. And after the threshold is crossed to a certain extent, it then becomes clear what the immediate meaning element is in reality: it is the light in which the angels sense. True Spiritual Imagination takes place with the whole being, not just the head.

[56] *Ideas I*, p 63

A) First, after closing the eyes, one can orient a primary ray of attention to a lower region of darkness in the field of the mind's eye, while a weaker second ray of attention is simultaneously oriented toward a 'higher' region. This higher region is expressing the concepts that one is thinking by means of unclear images. These vague images, which often have a character determined by the impressions of memory, are experienced as unfolding outside the field of inner vision, in a sense, 'behind' or 'beyond' the primary ray of intention. It is almost as if one were buried in dirt and looking into the dark surroundings with one's primary attention, while a barely functional periscope was turning around and surveying the air and light above the dirt. Another analogy might help. The experience of seeing someone's hand in front of one's face with external perception differs from the experience of feeling this same hand scratching one's back, in that the full perceptual features are lacking in the second experience. But both experiences relate to a perception of the hand. In the same way, when the primary ray of attention is oriented toward the lower region of darkness (or toward word strings) it is as if the weaker secondary ray of attention is 'seeing' the images with the same degree of obscurity that one perceives a hand scratching one's back. This is the sort of intuition of a representation or 'mental image' with which most people are familiar. It is for this reason that there has even been academic dispute about the image character of mental-pictures. Of course, most 'thinking' takes place while the eyes are open, and so the primary ray is usually oriented toward sense phenomena. This remains subjective.

B) Through inner effort and practice in precise visualization, one may shift the primary ray of attention toward the higher region described above. With concentration, a new sort of presentation of mental images becomes apparent in this region, which brings them into full relief as clearly 'seen' pictures. During the process of 'thinking' or during the explicit process of eidetic variation, one can then hold the images in view; it is the case that they now possess a subtle quality that can be *compared to* watching the images on a movie screen reflected in a stream of slowly moving water. In this second case, the categorial intuition of the mental images is more like perceiving the hand out in front of one's face, or shifting the primary attention to a fully functional periscope above the ground. Some people experience hypnogogic images which unfold precisely in this region and manner. This remains subjective.

C) To reach Husserl's logical vision it is necessary to go one step further. In the phenomenological shift, which orients itself in order to register or grasp the eidos itself, a second ray of attention must move toward an examination of what is trying to assert itself through (or beyond) the images that are being transformed by the primary ray. The eidos stands forth as a *proto-structural principle* especially clearly when the primary ray of attention (in situation B) begins to retreat into the background by dropping the persistent tendency of the mind to insert images from remembered experience into this mold or prototype. This is a form of eidetic reduction, in which the presuppositions about what should appear as the essence are dropped, and the inherent biases present in the self are partially set aside. By setting some of the presuppositions out of play, the essence is allowed to self-present its own ideal formal and dynamic element without residue or remainder.[57] This reduction then allows the phenomenological researcher to stand in "a world of absolutely pure possibility."[58] This virtual field has an immediate light character and an immediate meaning element within every little eddy or stream of it. The particulate flowing mental image shifts on its own, as it arises out of the imageless concept of immediately understood meaning 'behind' it. But now one sees the tendency of meaning or interpretation that is active, like understanding why you see the cloud in the sky as now a dragon, now a turtle, now a spaceship.

In my experience, this world of pure possibility shows different qualities than the normal field in which noematic images are perceived (in the clearly

---

[57] It must be repeated that this is not yet Spiritual Imagination in Steiner's sense, because the basic double bind of the Ahrimanic and Lucifer enclosure and the bubble of subjectivity are still fully operational. This is a region where great self-delusion can arise in the path of spiritual development of the new etheric scientific clairvoyance. Only the moral opening of the heart can lead to true Imagination. Then one passes outside of this first grid.

[58] Husserl, *Phenomenological Psychology*, pgh 9. Quoted in Sokolowski p 62

evident 'higher region' in situation B). This step-C experience is made of an illuminated, malleable substance, and displays a coordinate of 'grids' stretching in many different dimensions, that can analogously be compared to the illustrations of curving space in Lobachevskian geometry.

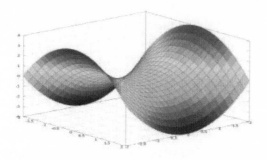

"A hyperbolic paraboloid, which is the surface described by the hyperbolic geometry of Lobachevsky. The edges are illusions: the surface extends forever." [59]

This 'game board' is filled with repetitive streams of colors, and tiny elements that can take on a variety of forms, perhaps like some of Kandinsky's paintings. This malleable substance seems to naturally take on shapes and impressions, as if it were the film receiving the impressions of light in an analog camera. It is obvious that such a vision inspired Harris' illustration of the essential components of the second degree of

---

[59] From Matthew Francis' science blog

Freemasonry that ends this chapter. It might be worthwhile to ponder this connection further. This is not yet the soul experience of the astral watery-light that Steiner calls the strata of mobile or flowing sensitivity (*fließende Reizbarkeit*), but it is instead made up of the dying grid of the reproduction of form in the etheric formative forces entering and surrounding the head.[60] The grid is like the freezing crust of the elemental forms of the 4 ethers that pre-exist in the etheric world. To move beyond this and cross into the soul and spiritual worlds, one must deal with the moral exposure of the impersonal fields which threaten to snuff out all sense of individuality, sense, and wakefulness. One has to behold the monsters that live in oneself, to truly perform the 'spiritual reduction' (could we call it level D? Yet the linear progression must end at level C). Of course, in Husserl's sense, it would also be possible to perform an intuition of the eidos with the physical eyes remaining open, but the entire process becomes tainted by the overpowering influx of percepts from the external world. Regardless, this is a problem that has to be solved individually by each serious spiritual scientific researcher. I have to become the one who can both make and dissolve the forms.

Steiner also often suggested using a type of imaginative variation to grasp the universal or general concept as a mobile creative element:

---

[60] See Steiner, GA 9, chapter 2 for more on the astral water. Also refer to GA 141 and GA 183

But we can also take the triangle as a starting-point, and allow each side to move in various directions and at different speeds...in this way we really do lay hold of the triangle in its general form; we fail to get there only if we are content with one triangle. The general thought, 'triangle' is there if we keep the thought in continual movement, if we make it versatile.[61]

He indicates that through this transformation of the static forms of species into the underlying generative movement, one is able to penetrate into the living spiritual process that creates the individual forms. The pulsing flux, which is the mother of all triangles, can be seen in the same place where one sees concepts. Goethe, by using such a method, was able to discover the prototypes of plants and animals, which Husserl would call their eide. Husserl does seem to have been able to penetrate fully to level C, but he was focused more on the meaning elements, logical connections and formal ramifications, rather than the organic living power or image character of what was revealed. Steiner calls this noematic element or proto-structural flowing entity, "the living element which ramifies through the whole evolution of the animal kingdom, or the plant-kingdom, and creates the forms."[62] Yet, eventually there is some level at which the spirit of the triangle is just as living as the spirit of the flower. Thus, humans move in a living organic math as the plants grow in the life that underlies the Fibonacci stream. To cross into the spiritual world proper, one has to become the triangle

---

[61] Steiner, *Human and Cosmic Thought* (GA 151), lecture 1
[62] GA 151, same lecture

(and yet remain oneself). Then one can see the dying grid from the outside. Active forgetting, love of nature, and objective self-knowledge are wonderful tools to progress, as we will see in chapter 8.

Husserl and Steiner both agree that the concept of the triangle that you think of, is at bottom, the exactly identical one in the concept world that I think of. There is only one Washington Monument, likewise there is only one concept of leaf, zebra, circle, beauty, war, and so on. The psychologism that Steiner found in *Logical Investigations* became less prominent in the later Husserl. For Husserl, the eidos was the essential interior of the Washington monument. To think together is to plunge into the same ocean. Humans are able to comprehend that they are accessing the same essence in two different experiences. When we intuit the eidos of 'mammal,' or form the proposition '*The katydids are singing*' at two different times, a scrupulous awareness toward the original sense convinces us, with adequate evidence, of their identity. This numerical identity guarantees univocity of meaning, and thus the possibility of coherent communication altogether. Of course, the essence is not the representation and it is not grasped only in subjective thought. As the post-structuralists aptly demonstrate, this essential unity does not indicate that the meaning-life of the eidos cannot grow and change. It is virtually alive after all, and contains formlessness at the bottom of its spiritual roots. It is a pulsing formless self-differentiation that undergirds identity. Only I outside myself can know it and become it. But this différance is a positive phenomenon, since it allows you and I to create individual meaning elements and imaginative forms out of the identical-difference living in the underlying spiritual formlessness. Thinking is the feature that the formless Spirit creates in man, as Steiner points out. [63]

---

[63] The following quote from Steiner can itself solve every issue in understanding the relationship between Goethe and Husserl's experiences, and the nature of reality, "Every sensation, every impulse, which arises in an animal is brought forth from the foundations of the animal soul. The shape is more enduring than the feeling or impulse. One may say the sensation life bears the same relation to the more enduring living shape that the self-changing plant shape bears to the rigid crystal. The plant to a certain extent exhausts itself as the shape-forming force; during its life it goes on constantly adding new shapes to itself. First it sends out the root, then the leaf structure, then the flowers, etc. The animal possesses a shape complete in itself and develops within this the ever-changing life of feeling and impulses. And this life has its existence in the soul world. Just as the plant is that which grows and propagates itself, the animal is that which feels and develops its impulses. They constitute for the animal the formless which is always developing into new forms. Their Archetypal processes when traced to their primal source are found in the highest regions of "Spirit-land." But they carry out their activities in the soul world. There are thus in the animal world, in addition to the Force Beings who, invisible to the senses, direct growth and propagation, others that have descended into the soul world, a stage still deeper. In the animal kingdom formless Beings, who clothe themselves in soul sheaths, are present as the master builders, bringing about sensations and impulses. They are the real architects of the animal forms. In theosophy one calls the region to which they belong the Third Elementary Kingdom. Man, in addition to having the capacities named as those of plants

From Steiner we discover that there are other beings, forces, and active elements that can be spiritually seen that exist beyond what Goethe or Husserl were able to intuit. The etheric, astral, and spiritual worlds are full of elements and beings that become slowly apparent to the spiritual researcher.

---

and animals, is furnished also with the power of working up his sensations into ideas and thoughts and of controlling his impulses by thinking. The thought which appears in the plant as shape and in the animal as soul force makes its appearance in him in its own form as thought itself. The animal is soul; man is spirit. The Spirit Being, which in the animal is engaged in soul development, has now descended a stage deeper still. In man it has entered into the world of sensible matter itself. The spirit is present within the human sensible body. And because it appears in a sensible garment, it can appear only as that shadowy gleam or reflection which the thought of the Spirit Being affords. The spirit manifests in man through the apparatus of the physical brain mechanism. But at the same time it has become the inner being of man. The animal feels and moves as it chooses, but exhibits no thoughts. Thought is the form which the formless Spirit Being assumes in man just as it is shape in the plant and soul in the animal. Consequently man, in so far as he is a thinking being, has no Elementary Kingdom constructing him from without. His Elementary Kingdom works in his physical body. Only in so far as man is shape and sentient being, do Elementary Beings work at him in the same way as they work at plants and animals. The thought organism of man is developed entirely from within his physical body. In the spirit organism of man, in his nervous system which has developed into the perfect brain, we have sensibly visible before us that which works on plants and animals as supersensible Force Being." GA 9

Furthermore, as we cross from the elements of color and form, and begin to see ourselves objectively from the outside with all of our moral failings and instinctual motivations, we must first begin to read the colors and forms of the spiritual world, but then begin to set them aside altogether. We are also split into an apocalyptic zodiacal multiplicity. Steiner says the following in his esoteric lessons, which must be received in a gentle and open way, in order to truly begin to understand and experience of what he speaks:

> The spiritual world is first of all, completely colorless, lightless, soundless and so on. All the colors we see, for example, are not spiritual, but come from our own inner being, and they indicate those qualities which we do not yet have, which we still have to attain. If, for example, we see a red color, it means that we do not yet have love in us, that we have to develop it in ourselves. If we see purple, it means that we must acquire devotional piety. When we hear tones like earthly sounds, it is not something spiritual, but something that comes from ourselves. If someone has an appetite for a certain food, for example, or if someone starts to eat vegetarian food, but still has the inner, bodily inner desire for meat, even if he does not become aware of it, this appetite sounds out in tones, in discordant tones. All these tones and sounds are only the occult crowing of ravens! If a figure from earlier times appears to the disciple and he wants to interpret it in the same way, it is completely wrong. He must be able to wait with the interpretation. The pupil should not interpret in the present, but only later. If such an image comes before our soul, it is destroyed as soon as we come

up with our thoughts. But if it is a real picture, it will appear again later and then rest in its true form, and we will know what it means. But we must be able to wait, wait and be silent. Just as we ourselves should not approach the experiences with our own thoughts, we should talk about them much less. We should consider and treat our whole spiritual life as something sacred. With all these experiences of sounds and colors and so on we must tell ourselves that they do not come from the spiritual, but from our own inner being, from our own self, which receives waves from the sea of desires and passions, as Noah's Ark was propelled by waves over the sea. And we must live in the conviction that all these experiences and appearances are not spiritual. By saying this very clearly and relentlessly to ourselves, we must, as it were, surrender our ego, give up the desire of our ego to experience content, to let it fly away, as the dove was let away from Noah's Ark and did not return. But then another occult experience of the disciple comes later. When we have realized that there is nothing, nothing spiritual about those experiences of sounds and colors, when we have realized with inner strength that the spiritual world is completely empty for us, then we realize that those experiences have a meaning after all, a meaning for ourselves. The colors come to warn and advise us then; they tell us what we do not yet have, what we still have to achieve. From the tones we recognize that they reflect bodily desires. And when the images that we have calmly let work tell us their meaning, then the soul is enriched by such experiences. This is like the second dove that was sent forth from the Ark and returned with the olive branch, the symbol of peace.[64]

---

[64] GA 266b p 73-74

Tracing board for the 2nd Degree of Freemasonry by Frieda Harris

109

Chapter 5 – From Earthly Logic to Spiritual Imagination

What is a Proposition?

Now that we have given a deep overview of Husserl's work and some of its limitations, as well as surveyed some of the revelations of spiritual science from Steiner, let us focus on a variety of more specific questions, riddles, and problems concerning thinking, meaning, logic, and real life. We shall plunge into the depths of the logical process and the nature of meaningful expression itself. The term 'proposition,' means something that is placed down in front, or set forward, in its original Latin form. Great controversies surround every philosophical concept and this one is no exception. The confusion arises once again from the different ways that we understand and inwardly perceive what is happening when we think. Generally, all parties could agree that what is indicated by the statement, "Pemberton surrendered Vicksburg to Grant on July 4, 1863" is a proposition. This statement, fact, or idea is what all parties believe to be true about the events that we experience in the world. But the same idea could be expressed in other alphabets, other languages, smoke signals, or in symbolic logic. So, it is obviously not the particular expression in English that is the object of all of our particular belief about this event in the American Civil War. Traditionally, in accordance with the writings of

Boethius (6th c), a '*propositio*' was an expression either mental or spoken of something that was either true or false. If you belong to the camp that believes that all of your mental processes are just abstractions from sense experience, then it seems obvious that two people who agree about this fact of the Civil War are not agreeing about the truth of the particular pale reflection that I hold in my personal head about 1863. Such thinkers believe that since different people have different individual thoughts (they sometimes call them 'mental tokens') and may often be mistaken, it is absurd to expect that truth could be based on the pale shadows that we hold of sense experience in our psychological states. To this camp, it is obvious that some sort of objective truth exists (usually concrete material states) and that we believe in this objective reality beyond our thinking. All propositions are expressions that refer to these objective material processes. To solve this problem, such people imagine that some sort of scheme of independent verification of truth would have to take place that would not be based on personal states of belief. It would have to be a non-human mechanism. The history of modern logic has been an attempt to establish this mechanism for independently and objectively securing the verification of the facts about reality.

But throughout the longer history of logic reaching back to the Greeks, it has been the case that propositions were considered to be members or parts of the flow of reasonable thought that was expressed in language. 'S is p' is the universal formula for a proposition, uniting a 'subject' like Grant with a 'predicate,' quality, or characteristic about Grant, such as 'he accepted the surrender of Pemberton and his troops at Vicksburg.' All of the philosophical discussions about the general organization and legitimate structures of reasonable thought were, throughout the history of logic until the late 19th century, demonstrated by reference to different configurations of 'propositions.' In brief, they set up combinations of propositions like this - 'All wizards wear pointy hats. Gandalf is a wizard. Therefore, Gandalf wears a pointy hat.' The combination of propositions is traditionally called a syllogism. One can pursue this history and all of its details further. What is important for us here is the following.

There are also other camps who look at the question of 'how is the assertion that I make in thinking or speaking related to the objective truth of the world?' in different ways. First of all, there are serious problems with imagining that all true statements or thoughts just refer to material events in a real world. This becomes glaringly apparent when we consider more closely our assertions about Grant. How am I to verify this belief? It happened in the past and no one who is alive now witnessed it. It is no longer a material event like the fact that I currently own and drive a Mazda. Is the reference of my belief the statements written in books about the Civil War? Where is the region where this objective reality exists? It is certainly not in the paper of the books themselves! Likewise, it may be true that I followed a reasonable line of thinking and did not contradict myself or make a logical slip in my syllogism about wizards. But what and where is the target of my reference to Gandalf, who is a fictional character? Is Gandalf just the sum of the letters in the Roman alphabet that Tolkien used in his books? It seems like this example shows me that I can use the apparatus of thinking correctly and consistently, even if the particular content of the statements is fictional. The bigger problems for logic lie in other directions. If material events that are observed can never be false, and all propositions ultimately refer to material events, how is it possible to utter a false statement at all, or believe in something that is false? What is the degree of reality of a false statement? And so on.

Some logicians have argued that just like geometrical axioms and numbers seem to exist independently of our psychological states, and we can hold very accurate truths about them, which also follow pretty lock-tight trails of reasoning, then there is also a realm of true notions about reality that we also refer to when we believe in something, speak about something or hold assertions about something. This camp still tries to remain in a grey area which does not dive into metaphysical commitments about a realm of eternal or divine truth like the idealists do. Even though people like Frege ultimately lead logic into a totally different direction than Husserl and Steiner (specifically, to the symbolic logic undergirding modern computation), he also maintained a belief in some sort of ultimate propositions which exist outside of our particular thinking about them. So did Bolzano, who had a large influence on Husserl. But, in the end, the camp that we are interested in following here, and the camp that I am a member of, inches much closer to the traditional Idealist one. As we have already seen, Husserl will say that the evidence of truth is given securely in a realm of concepts that one can dive into and see directly. Truth is revealed in thinking, and elements that can be thought can also be directly experienced as evidence.

Since all claims about what is true in human experience are based on an elaboration of evidence through the fundamental laws of logic, which are in turn grounded in the notion of the proposition in general, we need to understand what a proposition really is to establish this legitimate foundation for both the empirical and the spiritual sciences. Even scientific research that regards the empirical sphere as the sole source of legitimate data requires such a foundation, for the forms of logic do not somehow organize the external diversity of the natural world into meaningful knowledge by their own powers, but require human thinking to exercise their capacity to collect, order and understand. Furthermore, logical laws themselves are not perceived in the way that I perceive the colors of a sunset, so some form of abstraction from sensible contents into laws of thought must be necessary. This is also a human endeavor. A groundhog could certainly have perceived Pemberton surrender to Grant, but it surely created no hypotheses about its effects, or even uttered any meaningful statements about the event at all. The more complex question today can focus on to what extent an artificial intelligence can make meaningful

114

statements about reality. Will a cyborg from the 23rd century be thinking about true events in the same way that humans experience truth in their thinking today? I doubt it. To organize data into meaningful units and to provide the interpretation of the quantitative results of objective experimentation also requires the use of human reasoning, which itself rests on the fundamental question of this section of the chapter. Husserl describes his phenomenological understanding of the nature of the proposition quite clearly here:

> A proposition, especially, for example, a truth, is something suprasubjective, supratemporal, ideal, [while] an act of thinking, [is] something subjective, temporal, and psychologically real. How does the ideal come into the real, the suprasubjective into the subjective act? The judgment judges that S is P, that the sum of the angles <is equal> to the sum of two right <angles>, etc. The what of the judgment is the judgment content. Is that a moment, an isolated feature of the judgment, as green is an isolated feature in the appearance of green leaves? But, with the real whole, its real parts, its real moments also come into being and pass away. If the green leaf passes away, then that moment of coloration has passed away. If the judgment passes away, then everything that constituted the judgment in terms of parts or isolated features has passed away. The

proposition is, however, what it is, whether it is thought or not.[65]

We see that Husserl is trying to push beyond the limits of subjectivity in this quote, trying to find the realm of Truth's happening. Although Husserl penetrates into the realm of 'self-evident truth' exhibited during the intuition or direct seeing of concepts as they are combined into 'suprasubjective' propositions, Steiner goes much further even than Plato in his description of the ultimate reference of meaning. Steiner in his role as an Initiate, discloses that all reference to truth is ultimately a reference to the activity and life of spiritual beings. All thought is, when it is experienced in its deepest reality, the activity of human beings working together with spiritual beings. This is the highest stage of Spiritual Intuition proper. He says, "In a certain sense, each spiritual being speaks to the soul in its own way. A spiritual interchange thereby arises that consists of a language of thoughts. You experience thoughts, but you know that you experience beings in those thoughts. To live in beings that do not merely express themselves in thoughts but are present in them with their own being: that is what it means for your soul to live in the spiritual world." He also says, "The soul has the feeling that cosmic thought does not simply radiate into these spiritual beings, but that their being lives in that interweaving of thoughts. They allow cosmic thought to think and live in them completely.

---

[65] *Introduction to Logic and Theory of Knowledge* (Lectures 1906/7), p 131

Their life unfolds in the perception of the language of cosmic thought. Their will consists of making themselves manifest in the form of thoughts. Their existence in thought, in turn, has a significant effect upon the universe. Thoughts that are beings speak with other thoughts that are also being. Human thought-life is a reflection of the life of these spiritual thought-beings."[66]

The spiritual researcher today, following in the path of Steiner can confirm and experience the truth of these findings. A growing number of people like the author have glimpsed the first opening of this confirmation today. When we look into the world of colors and forms with our eyes, and see the beauty of a graceful, curving plant, wrapped in a white bark, interspersed with black, rising tall into the air, our thinking immediately finds the concept of a birch tree, and unites it with our perception, to give us a feeling of the whole of earthly reality and knowledge.[67] But

---

[66] *A Way of Self-Knowledge* (GA 16)

[67] The flip side of this activity is that there is a luciferic spirit who takes some of the light from the spirit being in the concept world, and pulls it down, giving it over to the ahrimanic spirit, who solidifies it with the record-needle activity taking place in the pineal gland. On the other side, the ahrimanic spirit in us, projects an electric grid of dead will out into the warm fields of colored light that live in the real spirit world, and he freezes this into a mental picture. He consolidates this through the connection of the pineal and pituitary gland (where the 'needle' writes on the 'record,' so to speak), and he hands over the mental picture to the luciferic spirit. At the same time, our spiritual sense of will and balance, and our spiritual life in the midst of the world, is cut off from below our consciousness, and

can we also look, feel, and will in the interior of the invisible region where the concept of a birch tree is a living process, creativity of meaning, woven by the life of the spiritual world? Can we feel the sense of truth in our experience of intuition or direct perceiving of the land of concepts in their moment by moment unrolling of life? Can we go further to gently ask the blessing of the kindly spirit of the Birch tree to meet us in a move of self-conscious devotion?

The proposition in its entire truth consists of a wide variety of different aspects, which are understood and perceived in varying degrees of consciousness. The proposition can be expressed through outer speech, such as, "That tree on the hill is a birch." The meaning is projected outward by a mixture of internal meaning and intention with the speech organism's mastery of specific shapes of air. This external form permits another being to understand the internal state of soul of the speaker by the transferal of the meaning-shape and the object of reference itself. The speaker certainly does not need to turn her regard to the inner constituents of the process of meaning-formation nor the eidetic features of the ideal referent in order to express a proposition meaningfully.

---

the feeling of the interiority of the subjective consciousness is created. We believe that external objects exist as physical objects and we live in the quantitative earthly consciousness. Ben-Aharon has clarified this in many different ways in his teaching and written works. See *The New Experience of the Supersensible* for more details.

But there is an aspect to our symbolic thinking and our thinking in a single language in words and writing, which has nothing to do with the life of color and form that we see, nor the rough or soft surfaces we touch, nor the unfolding of meaning in the conceptual landscape in which we think. And there is also the way in which the world uses language to speak beyond our intention, through us. The world speaks the word through us and who knows what the other may hear or interpret or feel in our speech, if the divine source of that word is heard in its spiritual light, warmth, and life? Can we hear the spiritual mantric gestures lying in the depths of PRO - PO - SIT - IO? Can we live in the fire that burns beneath at the root before even this mantric gesture rises? The highest degree of Modus Ponens reveals itself here (and remember that *ponere* and *positus* are different forms of the same Latin word, which underlies *propositio*) – God created me and therefore I AM. I am placed down from God; I am a living proposition. The Word created me.

Yet one may also attend in phenomenological reflection to the process of thought as it rings in the internal sound of silent speech. Here we discover that the whispering voice of inner speech indeed utters the distinctly English proposition, "That tree on the hill is a birch." At the same time, we can sense as inner-feeling the slight motion of the possibility of speaking such a proposition externally and audibly in the area of the larynx, as if the speech organism was continually practicing for the ever-present necessity of voicing any individual thought. One may then turn

119

a ray of consciousness upward toward the upper head region, moving the inner attention away from the mental expression of this proposition as a specifically English construction and toward the idea or meaning behind the grammatical arrangement. Whereas the specific linguistic arrangement of the idea in English is propagated through the proto-tonal strata of the nexus of formative forces, the meaning in the average inner reflection on its constitution as pure thought is expressed through the strata of generative or vital forces, through the life-ether. And its spiritual meaning dies in my nervous system, but I live from its death.

It is one thing to describe meeting the spirit of the birch tree in language or in an abstract thought, floating like a miniature crust inside our head, organized in our brain. It is quite another to discover and struggle with the moral riddle, anxiety and problem of actually meeting the spiritual world, and creating concepts out of this meeting. It requires a moral step, and a hearty self-knowledge, which clearly recognizes the possibility that I would simply use this knowledge to benefit my personal self or to simply feed off of the life of the spirit, without really transforming my consciousness and my actions. Do I really only want to expand my personal ego to vast world stretches, spreading the love of my personal self everywhere? What am I really grasping for in my desire for spiritual experience? Each person must learn to wipe the smile from his face as he becomes the abyss. Husserl only went so far in his experience, because he never found this true passageway beyond death into the realm of truth. He always stops at a certain boundary. All of us have our limits.

In this way we see that what one means is not an internal copy or organized mental feature abstracted from sense-perception, but rather a meeting as thought-being with what manifests itself through human perception as an individual birch tree that is spatially determined. The blossom of the spiritual archetype blows its life into the new petals of my concept life. One understands that the meaning of the proposition is concerned with the virtuality of the being of the birch tree. Understanding full reality means to stand in the midst of spiritual and soul beings, living a life independent of you, but also morally interwoven with you. What appears in external nature is the same being that is met in the spiritual world and in the proposition; this ultimate referent is at least partially conveyed. One day we will hear its true name. It is only through spiritual scientific research, in which we have been educated through Rudolf Steiner and Yeshayahu Ben-Aharon, that we can also carefully watch how real spiritual meaning dies into us, becoming a frozen crust, and an electro-neural web in our brain and body. We can become more aware of the transition zone between our personal desire of meaning and the world reality in spirit and soul, and the transition zone where spiritual life becomes symbolized, deadened, and shrunken. After it is fully paralyzed, it then emerges as the little fairy movie, broadcast in miniature onto the screen of the interior of my skull.

But how do we learn to remain awake in the zone where we kill the spirit in thinking, and how do we remain awake as we are thought by the light of the spiritual hierarchies? Can we bring the activity of polarizing and intensifying into the very transformation of our soul, stretching out, diving in? Can our I become so flexible and gentle and humble that it can become free in the middle? Only the Good Master knows the path of dying and resurrection. First, when a human being attempts to become actively aware of the deepest inner aspects of his thinking, he may reorient the self-reflective ray of his attention toward the conscious formation of meaning in its syntactically arranged container of human language. In the midst of this reflective or phenomenological route, one may become aware of the fact that the linguistic container is permeated by pure thinking, or a forward flow of grammar shapes which stand at a higher or more primordial level. But both of these are different layers of crystalline architecture in the subjective and dying part of the human soul. The fact that I see them means that I am becoming alive. The level of pure grammar or the transformation of meaningful structures that are not yet an individual language (such as English), is itself usually unconscious. Out in the cosmos, it lives in the spiritual revelation of the constellations and planets themselves. It is part of the Super-Logic in which we live at night. It is beyond earthly and transcendental logic. If one penetrates to the sphere in which one experiences that the hierarchical Spirit-Beings are dwelling in activity inside the structure of pure thinking, and human meaningfulness, then the content of one's thinking is wholly transformed. In reverence and devotion, we are flipped inside out. This opens up a meeting zone or a creative space where, if the moral problems of death and evil in the human being are seen at all (which means if the work of the ahrimanic and luciferic and zorathic spirits are recognized at all, as they work inside our very own soul and structures of consciousness, where they act through us), then we can find something that is totally new at every moment in the life of our thinking. We can negotiate new spiritual-earthly meaning with our angelic co-workers. This is the task of our time, to become adept in this practice. But our very self must be transformed, and we should not just receive revelation from other beings, but we must bring a gift of our earthly experience to the table, to be used and transformed through our co-working. Lower logic becomes Higher logic in cosmic moral cognition. Here thinking becomes a moral-cognitive artistry and free creation, controlled by the meeting of the earthly self with the spiritual I-AM working inside our egos. But this requires recognizing the I as an activity or an exhalation-inhalation cognitive-perceptive stream of becoming earthly and becoming divine, moment to moment. I see myself from the inside looking out, I become the world-self looking in from the outside. And in this process, I have guides and co-workers in earthly life and spiritual life. And Christ is the guide of the creation and merging of these various streams. Once again, Husserl could not enliven his logical categorial intuition with enough moral fiber and artistic creativity to cross the void of death, in order to experience the resurrected life of spiritual thinking from the other side. In a spiritual and soul logic, linking with Husserl's transcendental logic, we can find a moral life of spiritual and soul love. Provided we never forget the un-ending apocalyptic holocausts living in the ground of our human history on the Earth. It must be engraved in the center of our heart, as we read in *The Spiritual Event of the 20th Century*. And that book is also alive.

How do we experience the moment of making any judgment whatsoever? This is one of the main questions of Husserl's *Formal and Transcendental Logic*. We find that if we follow this through to the soul and spiritual levels, we can see that any judgment can be a marriage of the spiritual I with the soul vehicle, where the creative life of the spiritual will is imprinted on the fabric of the receptive soul garments. Each judgment is in reality a gentle wedding of spiritual and soul. We then take a formal extraction from the imprints on this soul garment and pull it into a structure that is shrunken into a localized size, into our feeling of being inside the interior of a body, and we store a dead, frozen image of this soul imprinting in, like a drawing of a dead leaf in our brain and body. In our normal consciousness, we call the manipulation of these drawings of dead leaves 'thinking' or propositions. That is our job in the 21st century, to connect all of the dots without shame or blame.

How do we cut a track in the snow from our brain-thinking to this other sort of soul experience, the soul and spiritual wedding, and the creative working? This is one method, which is characterized clearly in

Ben-Aharon's work: we can take this examination of the intentional process of meaning one step further. As we will discuss in more detail later, it is then possible to repress and negate the clarity of the mental picture along with its linguistic element as well as the light forms present in the head region. When one actively forgets and erases this active central clarity in the intentional zone, and opens up a patient and peripheral attentive which waits for what is alive in thinking to arise, it can be that one begins to feel an entire field of circumferential warmth that surrounds the previous clarity of intentional mental images, forms, and linguistic connections. But all of this must be poured down with love, wonder, devotion and faith into the heart and body.

Because there is a natural moral content to this new sphere of Living-Thought, the intention to express an inner experience through meaningful transference in thought is sublated into a devoted piety of interaction with cosmic deeds of being. And on the other side, I am wakened from death. In other words, if one redirects one's attention toward the ultimate reference to each utterance or sketch of thought, one can no longer simply spout off nonsensical trivialities or conduct external business as usual. The spirit-self wakes and lives and thinks in the midst of vast concept beings. I think myself from the inside out. Therefore, in the new awareness of enlivened thinking, there is not simply a manipulation of Spiritual Beings into typical boxes of abstract expression or practical verbalization by the human being alone, but there is a deep interaction between the Active Beings of Ideal Thought and the human thinker. Yet this can only be a strong mode of opening the heart (the Spiritual Logical Rule of Modus Cordis, or spiritual heart implication) and the soul and spiritual will, with a mood of devotion, reverence and even powerlessness. There is a grace that is involved in this process, and it cannot really be forced. We can try to do our best to elevate our thinking to the shepherd of spirits, but this means to try to meet what is highest in my sister and my Self. The right moral mood is established, if it is not forced, but in which an opening is made for the spiritual and soul world's activity to approach you, when the time is right. I spiritualize my thinking through a new Modus Re-Tollens, lifting up and de-actualizing all of the little ideas. The spiritual Biconditional Introduction (P $\leftrightarrow$ Q) is the new conversation arising between the spiritual world and man, in every thought. The higher self becomes the lower self, and the lower self becomes the higher, with the real gap of self-conscious death in the middle. The meaning of this Event governs all derivative propositions. Deleuze correctly states, "What renders language possible is the event insofar as the event is confused neither with the proposition which expresses it, nor with the state of the one who pronounces it, nor with the state of affairs denoted by the proposition."[68]

We could see that a future community can arise, where we see that every communication with another human using thinking and language, is also taking

---

[68] *Logic of Sense* p 182

place in a crowded space full of spiritual beings, with their own world-moods, intentions, and work. Not every spiritual being has the success of the human project as their central concern, so this is where our human freedom, nourished by the Spiritual-I of humanity at the center, can keep us balanced. We maintain earthly consciousness, but add on to it another form of etheric consciousness, with includes the life and thinking, feeling, and willing, and the interactions with the spiritual and elemental beings at their heart. This is what Ben-Aharon means when he shows us how the Event can be at the heart of our new communities. Every meaning is made new on each new day, and the earth's body and the human body is re-created with each sunrise. And we can contribute to the formation of this new futural day.

Chapter 6 – From Nature to the New Event – Studies in Spiritualizing Logic

A. Schönberg, *Denken*, 1910

Study 1. The Christmas Cactus and the Silky Dogwood Berry. Intuition, Imaginative Variation and the Experience of Truth

Let us once again begin from a state of normal consciousness and perception. In our anthroposophical work we can always start from the clearest self-consciousness, accurate observation, and strict and controlled thinking. From there, we can find our way into Husserl's realm of transcendental meaning life, and then demonstrate the difficult final step and twist into spiritual scientific insight. The old shriveled form of the Silky Dogwood berry from last autumn is tiny and nearly black. I perceive it before me, with its thin brown stem extending behind. Beside it the pink, maroon, and dirty white of the curled, dried out petals of the Christmas Cactus blossom is quiet and still. What prejudices, presuppositions, and old thoughts are functioning half-consciously as I perceive the decaying forms of plants? Am I a machine bot resonating in electric consciousness inside a skin, interpreting frequencies as photon data, upside down in retinal space? Am I a Bio-factory-pump? Am I rising angel wings soaring away from all matter in the bliss of inner beauty?

Can I set those old ideas aside and focus on the tiny changing qualities of the perceptions themselves? But this requires real love. Is there an unknown whisper in a cave of my heart in the center that has been forgotten? Where is the splintered heart in this disruptive discord, this *coup de coeur,* sensing the pulses of blossom and berry?[69] Can I also fade to

---

[69] Husserl, APAS p 362 "If the disruptive discordance has been overcome..." But what chords should we play in spiritual scientific research? Cacophony and dissonance

black, melting into the volcanic ash color of the berry, with its barky stem? Can I twist in magenta with the blossom of cactus? The colors gush into me, where I used to be. I am awake. No inner, no outer; all is water and air. All is earthly surging hope, in the robust life of pure sensation, and moral inward living color. Yet I am awake and listening.

When I lift the profiles I am living with in this moral color ocean and twist them in mental viewing, I can now see sides, versions, and types of berry and blossom never beheld with eyes before. I step into inward viewing in the transcendental turn. But I always know when stamen becomes stone, and pistil pistol. One bounces off elastic walls at the edges of meaning. There is a crack and a spark that runs like a fuse back behind all variable images in the limber fabric of iridescent fluctuation. Now comes the move to cross the great river. The drain hole beyond the eidetic leads to the moral friction of the I-AM who is always creating meaning. I am woken outside myself, morally, and by me Myself. But the gentle world living behind nature also wakes me. I make the transition from matter to extractive soul warmth: beyond crystal is liquid, beyond liquid is image, beyond image is pure motion, beyond pure motion is the formless emptiness,

---

can often separate figures of consciousness and regions of the soul in a way which allows to us to more precisely investigate and compare their different aspects with increased rigor and exactness.

130

and then the fire, creating free meaning out of the spirit-I, self-perceiving in world-balance.

When we listen to the message of the cactus blossom, we hear that it is disappearing and merging into the invisible, beyond its innocent sensuality. The silent tones of creative life speak in the local and in the world cosmic fields. The blackened outer crust of the berry is now fully dead, but in the center of its death, it holds the seed to new life, literally. I am now kneaded and shaped with it in ether fields. But its nourishment does not end at its spatial boundaries. In its split core, the mysteries of *coeur* and Koré live (one of the Mothers! Is it a little key?). I am de-nucleated in the moral heart of the Christ I that supports every element of my human being. My body holds the seed of the spirit, my spirit holds the seed of my body, as in Steiner's important mantra. And the I is born as the Son of Man, and the Son is born in the I of God.

The AND and the OR of space, the links between berry and blossom are put there by my I, thinking and weaving together with its concept-animals. Spiritual conjunction and disjunction are grown in ether life. Reason weaves the knowledge into platform wholes and whirling vertical concept planes, an archetypal meaning-zoo. This journey into the self-awareness inside categories is not a visible chain. It is an invisible thinking spider web. It is Deleuze and Guattari's never ending root systems, seen by the eyes of thinking-life.[70] Yet all the chemicals of my body

---

[70]See *1000 Plateaus.*

can become eyes and streams of meaning-unveiling –
the roots grow invisibly beyond the fingers, and weave
in moral self-grasping thinking forms. My thinking
becomes moral finger and toe rhizomes, propelled by
devoted hearts.[71]

In the light of the life of the pulsing and streaming
etheric atmosphere of the earth, if I follow the fuse and
the Derridean absencing-drain, I find the following. I
am turned inside out and experience that the living
spirit world varies me. Imaginative variation is turned
inside out, the world creates me, but I coordinate it
through the self-aware, balanced spiritual self, in head,
heart, limbs. The Cartesian limits are overcome - I am
Imaginatively varied, therefore I AM. Here the warm
and living repetitions and echoes of berries of every
sort stretch to infinity. Here petals and pistils are
warm fabrics of my life, blending in layers. Spirit-I and
human ego breathe one another in and out. This
happens before and at a deeper spiritual level than

---

[71] "We know nothing of our Karma because we always
think only with that most superficial of organs, our brain.
The moment we begin to think with our fingers — and just
with our fingers and toes we can think much more clearly
than with the nerves of the head — once we have soared up
to the possibility of doing so — the moment we begin to
think with what has not become entirely material, when we
begin to think with the lower man, our thoughts are the
thoughts of our Karma. When we do not merely grasp with
our hand but think with it, then, thinking with our hand we
follow our Karma. And even more so with the feet; when
we do not only walk but think with our feet, we follow the
course of our Karma with special clarity." Steiner GA 230,
Nov 11 1923

what is called 'physical respiration.' Here I can ask that the moral life of my heart would open, and I could be guided into the folds of the life of the cactus and the dogwood, becoming other while in myself. From this pulsing vantage seed, we look back at Husserl's accomplishments, his 'eidetic intuitions' and his hopes of a dimly glimpsed universal coordination of reasonable concepts organized in harmony (mathesis universalis).[72] We see them from the inside, the outside, and the 'round-side', and recognize their limitations as crystallized representations that were still contained within the limits of the soul that is dependent on the organic functions of the body. The eidetic forms are inscriptions, traced by thin lines of inner fire on the inner surface of the astral body. They begin to glow as they are understood in the last spark of light in the ether body. Here they sometimes take on geometrical forms and fluxes, but still on the interior of a membrane that receives the life, light, and meaning from the outside. In rising into subjective consciousness in the personality, they die and shrivel as mental image. Steiner describes this situation with

---

[72] But Michaelic mathesis universalis is co-working with Him as a shepherd of the spirits who are the reality of thinking; but now the human I can freely remain itself and also intuit and live and learn and co-work as the fourth hierarchy with these hosts – recognizing and separating Lucifer, Ahriman and Christ. To describe mathesis universalis as 'a priori ontology' is pure cowardice. It tries to hide from the shattering truth of the reality of a world-wide cosmic moral thinking, and the weaving together of man and angels in conscious, free, co-operation and evolution.

the precision coming from the faculty of spiritual scientific Inspiration:

> Within the organism, the I comes in contact with the lifeless substances which have been separated off and permeates them. So that our organism appears as having, on the one hand, its organic processes permeated by the I, the process, that is, containing the living substance, and of having also what is lifeless — or shall we say mineralized — in the organism permeated by the I. This, then, is what is always going on when we think. Aroused by sense-perceptions outside, or inwardly by memory, the I gets the upper hand over the lifeless substances, and — in accordance with the stimulation of the senses or of the memories — swings these lifeless substances to and fro in us, we might almost say makes drawings in us with them. For this is no figurative conception; this use of inorganic matter by the ego is absolute reality It might be compared to reducing chalk to a powder and then with a chalky finger drawing all kinds of figures. It is an actual fact that the ego sets this lifeless matter oscillating, masters it, and with it draws figures in us, though the figures are certainly unlike those usually drawn outside. Yet the I, with the help of this lifeless substance, does really make drawings and form crystals in us — though not crystals like those found in the mineral kingdom. What goes on in this way between the I and the mineralized substance in us that has detached itself as in a fine but solid state — it is this which provides the material basis of our thinking. In fact, to Inspired cognition the thinking process, the conceptual process, shows itself to be the use the I makes of the mineralized substance in the human organism. This, I would point out, gives a more accurate picture of what I have frequently described in

the abstract when saying: In that we think we are always dying, — What within us is in a constant state of decay, detaching itself from the living and becoming mineralized, with this the ego makes drawings, actual drawings, of all our thoughts. It is the working and weaving of the ego in mineral kingdom, in that kingdom which alone makes it possible for us to possess the faculty of thinking.[73]

Yes, it is true, Husserl was not just caught in older forms of psychologism. Yes, it is true, Husserl was not just describing an outdated Platonism, where the Ideas exist outside of human consciousness. But he was also stuck in this largely intellectual, crystalized middle zone. However, it is now possible to weave together, through the wide-open door developed by Rudolf Steiner and the life of the spirit of Anthroposophy and the work of Michael and Christ, to bring individual human wakefulness into the outer world of the Platonic Ideas. And the Ideas are walking around. The Human and the Ideas weave and create together in a new earth and new human. The new human also weaves out beyond his personal subjective soul body, which he now actively controls with his ever flexible and infinitely quick I-AM-thinker, who now knows that he creates the concepts of body, land, inner and outer. He surfs on all waves with a moral surfboard. In this way in-tuition is being tutored by the tutelary spirit, the spirit in my heart. I Am intuited therefore I Am.

---

[73] GA 209, lecture of 23 Dec 1921

If we now consciously return back down into the chalky outlines of eidetic cognition, and bury ourselves once again in the process of dying inside the head, we can follow Husserl's winding search for truth. He said in the *Logical Investigations* (1900): "Truth is of course only experience in the sense in which something ideal can be an experience in a real act. Otherwise put: Truth is an Idea, whose particular case is an actual experience in the inwardly evident judgment...The experience of the agreement between meaning and what is itself present, meant, between the actual sense of an assertion and the self-given state of affairs, is inward evidence: the Idea of this agreement is truth, whose ideality is also its objectivity."[74] Husserl helps us see and experience and living pulse of world-human life in the will of thinking. I first must become what is alive behind the scenes in the external world, then I freely craft my own concept out of its essence. But I can only become and breathe out into the etheric life of the world, if I can face the death of all of my hopes and inner wishes. I can only become what is outside myself, if my boundaries are broken up in powerlessness. Spiritual scientific evidence is a continuous rhythm of devotedly becoming the world, passing through the heart's life, and then looking back at all of our moral failures with gentle but firm objectivity. Then I take courage and dive back down in again, bringing new light and life into my empty heart, into my frozen brain. My whole body becomes a field and all of its multiple roots, welcoming the seeds from soul and

---

[74] LI, vol 1, pgh 51

spirit-land. Truth then becomes a weaving respiration of dying and being born. I become the mother of new fields of earthly love. The warmth and coldness of the heart's blood, then pulses throughout the streams, caverns, patterns of the cosmic solar and planetary system, in its soul and spiritual nature. I swallow the bread of the Spirit Word, and give back the earthly harvest from my whole soul.[75]

---

[75] Steiner says, "A clairvoyant sees the will-impulses of a man flashing like flames through his etheric body and raying into his astral body; and he sees the feelings as forms of light. But the thinking that is experienced by man in his soul as his own, and expressed in words, is only a phantom of thinking — as you will readily believe, because physical sound too is only a phantom of something higher. Words have their organ in the sound-ether; our thoughts underlie our words; words are forms of expression for thoughts. These forms of expression fill etheric space inasmuch as they send their vibrations through the sound-ether; 'tone' or 'sound' is only the shadow of the actual thought-vibrations. The inner essence of all our thoughts, that which endows our thoughts with meaning (*Sinn*), actually belongs; in respect of its etheric nature, to the life-ether itself...In the Lemurian epoch...the two higher kinds of ether were withdrawn from him [mankind]. That is the inner meaning of the passage where it is said that when, as a result of the Luciferic influence, men had become able to distinguish between good and evil (pictorially expressed as eating of the 'Tree of Knowledge'), the 'Tree of Life' was kept out of their reach...Thus thought and 'meaning' (*Sinn*) were withheld from the power of arbitrary human will and preserved for the time being in the world of the Gods, in order not to be given to man until a later time. Everywhere on the Earth, therefore, we can find individual men with individual feelings and individual impulses of will; but thinking is uniform everywhere and language is uniform among the several peoples...When Zarathustra, with his pupils around him, spoke of the realm of spirit, he could say: 'Out

What comes from this living moral intuition is that Truth is an ideal experience of a concordance between what is understood at the very self-conscious moment of self-intuiting thinking, which is self-given as steady evidence, and woven into the world without fantasy or projection of delusion stemming from the personal soul inwardness. As spirit, I think myself from the outside. In the light of memory, in the presence of love, and in the future of world-intuition, my complete soul and spiritual nature pulses and rotates. My spiritual-earthly pulse, bouncing out and back, happens before my breath. My breath is an outcome of this living and dying, moment by moment, as Steiner shows us.

---

of heaven there streams down warmth, or fire; out of heaven there streams down light. These are the vestments of Ahura Mazdao. But behind these vestments is hidden that which has not yet descended but has remained above in spiritual heights, casting only a shadow in the physical thoughts and words of men.' Behind the warmth and light of the Sun is hidden that which lives in tone or sound, in meaning, manifesting itself only to those who are able to see behind the light that which is related to the earthly word as the heavenly Word is related to the part of Life that was withheld for the time being from humanity. Hence Zarathustra said: 'Look upwards to Ahura Mazdao; see how He reveals Himself in the physical raiment of light and warmth. But behind all that is the Divine, Creative Word — and it is approaching the Earth!' What is Vishva Karman? What is Ahura Mazdao? What is Christ in His true form? The Divine, Creative Word!" (GA 114) *Luke*, lecture 7

Husserl required from truth the following aspects: an experience of primal givenness that is grasped without residue and a full saturation of the particular judgment stemming from the intuitive experience (or seeing the interior life of concepts in the 'essence-show'). We can find this experience, in the deepest sense, if we cross over the moral threshold, and allow the Spiritual Event of our time to teach us His new ways. If we do this, never forgetting the temptations of Lucifer and Ahriman on either side, we may experience what Steiner outlines in his introduction to the third degree of his new version of the Misraim Service: "From a point of view centered outside the human being, what was formerly the outer world ceases to exist for the senses. It becomes an inner experience, as were previously thoughts, feelings, and will impulses, and a quite new outer world arises. It is an outer world that appears like the thinking, feeling, and willing of spiritual beings experienced within oneself, just as one previously experienced one's own thinking, feeling, and willing within oneself. 'I Am' which was formerly only a thought-point, becomes a rich inner experience in which organically cooperating spirit beings develop their activity; this activity proceeds from a multiplicity and has as its goal a unity; and this unity is – the human being. One learns to know oneself from a viewpoint outside oneself."[76]

The new appearance of Christ in the etheric world teaches us this new breath. For Husserl, there were

---

[76] GA 265, *Freemasonry and Ritual Work* p 202

limits to the amount of disruption, inversion, tracing, and disappearance of essence that he could tolerate in his version of a rigorous eidetic science. But now phenomenology has passed through the fire of pure human evil in the Shoah. We have carried it through ourselves, as we stretched out in clouds of human time. And after all of the excellent work of Sartre, Derrida, Deleuze, Guattari, Foucault, Levinas, and Merleau-Ponty especially, we can now let a much richer, wider doorway open to the deeper origins of human experience, sensation and thinking. When we add the shocking life of pure differentiation into the shifting center, the disappearing origin and the warm periphery to any phenomenological investigation of the contours and planes of thinking, we can elevate Husserl. Then we grasp the electric sludge of the ahrimanic spirit in us, penetrate with consciousness right to its center, and plunge it into the fire of the heart with love made of spirit blood. It is resurrected as the new etheric clairvoyance (a self-conscious substance) necessary for our future development.

Steiner's work has made this possible and this anthroposophical knowledge drama has now been accomplished by Ben-Aharon and the present author, giving a way to spiritualize in our own time, the un-sprouted seeds that were planted by people like Lotze, Brentano, and Husserl.[77] In addition, the crafting of

---

[77] I have crossed the threshold through the narrow path of spiritual science, through the help of group work, and intense schooling in the reality of the *Philosophy of Freedom* and the halls of learning that pulse in *Knowledge of Higher Worlds*. I have begun to work on the first stages of Imagination, with glimpses

the intuitive organs by Fichte, can now be carried into the present and used in the full creation of a new sensible-supersensible human-artistic project of consciousness, soul, body, and spirit-I. We build this in order to contribute to the creation of the human and his and her community as a legitimate 4th spiritual hierarchy, working on the sun-earth. Each of us can craft her gem of new knowledge, which will shine on the brows of our future Mothers, like new silmarils. All of this is now guided gently by the work of Michael, Christ, and Vidar, and their co-workers. But all of this analysis of what was not accomplished in the past is not criticism, because it demonstrates that what failed in the past can be completed by others in the future. Husserl and Fichte can only rejoice in this new fact in their spiritual environment. Perhaps a dance and a smile are in order.

Study 2 – An Example of Earthly-Cosmic Inference and Metamorphic Judgment: the Pink Mimosa Tree and Its Entangled Beetles

Let us study and activate the logic of life, beginning with observing the wonderful creatures all around us in nature. If I begin with normal subjective

---

of Inspiration and Intuition, but I am just a beginner. I do not put myself on the same level as Ben-Aharon, and of course Steiner stands at a much higher level.

consciousness, I then must first activate my wakefulness as a self-aware I-who thinks. In this way the I is recognized, re-activated and fully intuited in its spiritually active place which is neither inside the body nor outside, but within the midst of world and human concepts. Steiner says, "We must first consider thinking quite impartially, without reference to a thinking subject or a thought object. For in subject and object we already have concepts formed by thinking."[78] But the neutral 'It Thinks' eventually wakes up into a self-creative point that is above and before every concept. I begin to unite my normal sense of ego with this creative I, but carefully noting the differences between the living I 'out there' and my dead ego, surrounded by crystallized representations, and enlivened by lucifer and ahriman's work inside my soul and life. The waking spiritual-I provides its own ground of validity, truthfulness, and value out of itself, like the most powerful and quickest concept on the scene. It is a concept, but a self-aware and self-created one; an actor and creator in a land of concepts that are, at first, intuited as not self-aware, that is, not separate beings. Eventually all the concepts come to life. Because each element in the world of thinking, knowledge, and concepts is connected with every other one – in other words, the world of thought is a whole – inference, deduction, induction, and abduction are possible and active. Empirical judgment is just as much dependent on this instant connectivity of the flexible multiplicity-ocean of the world of concepts. For example, I see an unknown flash in the

---

[78] *Philosophy of Freedom*, chapter 3

woods beyond and within 2 seconds I link a first
tentative concept to the percept - 'Is that a car driving
on that steep hill in the woods?' and then instantly
connect the second perceptual data – a screeching
sound - to the first flash and my recent experience and
knowledge of the date in the beginning of July. Still
within 3 seconds, I realize that it is not a car driving
in the woods, but rather a small firework exploding in
the sky in front of the woody hill.

In earthly logic it is the case that the forms of
logical inference can be valid without the content of
the logical expression being true. I can think from a
major premise to a conclusion in a valid way, but still
be in error. For example: All stone structures require
mortar in the joints. The Pont du Gard is a stone
structure, therefore it must have mortar in between
the stones. The logical form is correct, but the content
is false (since the Pont du Gard is built of stones so
carefully cut that mortar was not necessary).   In
contrast, when we begin to connect earthly logic in
everyday consciousness with a soul and spiritual logic,
we must move into the realm where the form
transforms itself into only the frozen singular moment
of a continually moving thinking-reality-Imagination.
As Steiner says, "To go beyond the realm of the
specific entities – i.e. of forms – they would find their
way to mental pictures which are in continual motion,
that is, in their thinking, they would come to a

realization of the realm of the spirits of Movement –
the next higher Hierarchy."[79]

Metamorphic thinking is therefore required and it
is also necessary to pass into an activity of thinking in
which, in order for the movement of inference to be
soul and spiritually true, its content must also be true.
When we pass into spiritual inference, the rhythms,
motions, and turning points must be as spiritually real
as the content of the thinking – its Imaginative process
is a spiritually essential aspect of the truth of its
essential living Mood.   This does not mean that no
errors exist in metamorphic thinking and spiritual
inference, but that the external form of the abstract
argument cannot verify the truthfulness of the
argument without human consciousness.

It should also be carefully pointed out that part of
this living motion is contained in the rhythmic process
of polarizing and intensifying life which is present in
the will activity that is at the root of self-actualized
thinking. I am a spiritual-I, united with the soul of the
world, and I am a humble human I, fully in my body
and able to think with empirical rigor. I can become
something beyond my subjectivity and my personality
in meeting the leaves, bark, blossoms, and pods of a
Pink Mimosa Tree, for example, but then can bring its
elements in a dying representation into the furrows of
the brain and everyday consciousness. It would be
impossible to move from one thought to another
without the will in thinking, and this will-force is a

---

[79] GA 151

144

rhythmic fiery pulse, which comes to expression just as much in the polarizing aspects of dialectical logic in thinking as in the polar opposites of the bipinnate arrangement of leaves on the *Albizia Julibrissin* or Mimosa tree. The cosmic process of withering and blooming is just as much present in human consciousness, thinking, feeling, and willing as it is in the forms of the thin petals or pods on the Pink Mimosa blossoms. This earthly-human-spiritually-cosmic living thought then helps us to recognize and extend our knowledge by recognizing the following: the Pitcher plant takes the fact that the beetles are attracted to the scent of the Mimosa one step further – they close in on the beetles and use them for nourishment. On the other hand, although the beetles seem to be paralyzed with ecstasy in the pink petals of the Mimosa, they can exit once again. Then one step further in the direction beyond the Mimosa, we see the blossom of the Rose of Sharon, for example, which permits the bee to enter and exit at will. The joy of the bee is several degrees lower than the ecstasy of the beetles in Mimosa. We can extend this organic cloud of thought to consider this morphology in the realm of human thinking as well, where one can become conscious of the full dying process inherent in mental representations. On one hand, it is used for Ahrimanic food or the dried-out stems of abstraction. On the other, self-aggrandizement and escape from the earth in ecstatic imaginations in Luciferic excessive thinking-feeling – used to nourish our luciferic angel. The ahrimanic-luciferic dyad is like an invisible Pitcher plant, where we die without knowing, dreaming that we are awake. Or we sleepily gorge ourselves in pretend 'soul development', like the beetles in the Mimosa nectar. If we can morally wake up, and start to crawl out of pitcher's pool, perhaps we can remain awake in the middle. We become like a self-conscious bee-flower, exiting in and out. In the center, then we can become both earthly and spiritual, controlling our own dying and living, representing and re-spiritualizing of the whole cosmic process of thinking, through Christ's resurrection action in our I, with a community of humans on the earth-becoming-sun. In this sense, the symbol of the Egyptian Scarab Beetle with the Sun above its head can have a new meaning in our times. But more than this, we behold our whole self as we are beheld by the zodiacal hierarchies. The Twelve Gods surround the self-conscious Scarab. Steiner says:

> Thus we find the connection between human and cosmic thoughts. Human thought is the regent of the brain; cosmic thought is such a regent that we belong with our whole being to that which it has to accomplish. Only, because in consequence of our karma it cannot direct its thoughts on to us all equally, we have to be constituted in accordance with its logic. Thus we men have a logic according to which we think, and so have the Spiritual Hierarchies of the cosmos their logic....As when we think, for example, "The lion is a mammal", we bring two concepts together to make a statement, so the Spiritual Hierarchies of the cosmos think two things together, Mysticism and Idealism, and we then say: "Mysticism appears in Idealism." Imagine this first as the preparatory activity of the cosmos. Then resounds the Creative Fiat, the

Creative Word. For the Beings of the Spiritual Hierarchies the preparatory act consists in the choice of a human being whose karma is such that he can develop a natural bent for becoming a mystical Idealist. Into the Hierarchies of the cosmos there is rayed back something that we should call a "thought", whereas for them it is the expression of a man who is a mystical Idealist. He is their "thought", after they have prepared for themselves the cosmic decision — "Let Mysticism appear in Idealism." We have now, in a certain sense, depicted the inner aspect of the Cosmic Word, of Cosmic Thought. What we drew in a diagram as "cosmic logic" represents how the Spiritual Hierarchies of the cosmos think. For example: "Let Empiricism appear in the sign of Rationalism!" and so on. Let us try to realize what can be thought in the cosmos in this way. It can be thought: "Let Mysticism appear in the sign of Idealism! Let it change! Let it become Empiricism in the sign of Rationalism!" Opposition! The next move on would represent a false cosmic decision. After verification, the thought is changed round. The third standpoint must appear: "Voluntarism in the sign of Dynamism." These three decisions, through being spoken over a period in the cosmic worlds, give the "man Nietzsche". And he rays back as the thought of the cosmos. Thus does the collectivity of the Hierarchies speak in the cosmos! And our human thinking-activity is a copy, a tiny copy, of it. Worlds are related to the Spirit or to the Spirits of the cosmos as our brain is to our soul. Thus we may have a glimpse into something which we ought certainly to look upon only with a certain reverence, with a holy awe. For in contemplating it we stand before the mysteries of human individuality. We learn to understand — if I may express myself figuratively — that the eyes of the Beings of the higher Hierarchies roam over the single individualities among men, and that individuals are to them what the individual letters of a book are to us when we are reading. This we may look upon only with holy awe: we are overhearing the thought-activity of the cosmos.[80]

---

[80] GA 151, lecture 4

Chapter 7 – Anthroposophical Apophantics: Spiritualizing Judgment and Logical Validity through the Event

Consistency and Judgments: The Relationships between the Edifice of the Thought-World as a Whole and the World of Perception

What is the maternal unity of the wholeness of the thought world? What is the glue that allows it to fit together? Is there a magnetic attraction and repulsion which pulls certain areas together and pushes others apart? How does a new idea appear? Husserl says in *Formal and Transcendental Logic* :

> In such inquiry one is not yet concerned with the truth of the judgments but is concerned merely with whether the judgment-members included in a whole judgment, no matter how simple or complex it may be, are 'compatible' with one another or contradict one another and thereby make the

whole judgment itself a contradictory judgment, one that cannot be made 'properly.'[81]

Steiner describes the wholeness of the 'edifice of thoughts':

> The perception forces itself in upon us from outside; thinking works itself up out of our inner being. The content of this thinking appears to us as an organism inwardly complete in itself; everything is in strictest interconnection. The individual parts of the thought-system determine each other; every single concept ultimately has its roots in the wholeness of our edifice of thoughts. At first glance it seems as though the inner consistency of thinking, its self-sufficiency, would make any transition to perception impossible. If the statements of thinking were such that one could fulfill them in only one way, then thinking would really be isolated in itself; we would not be able to escape from it. But this is not the case. The statements of thinking are such that they can be fulfilled in manifold ways. It is just that the element causing this manifoldness cannot itself then be sought within thinking. If we take one of the statements made by thought, namely that the earth attracts all bodies, we notice at once that the thought leaves open the possibility of being fulfilled in the most varied ways. But these are variations that can no longer be reached by thinking. This is the place for another element. This element is sense perception. Perception

---

[81] FTL p 53-54. We will discuss his consequence-logic in further detail later.

affords a kind of specialization of the statements made by thoughts, a possibility left open by these statements themselves.[82]

We find that Husserl is focused on discovering the active law which controls the internal consistency of a group of conclusions that have been thought through. Steiner shows that every concept is linked to the wholeness of the thought world, but he also shows how the robustness of the elements of what is sense-perceptible leads us beyond the world of pure thinking. Let us investigate this carefully. A judgment often takes the form, S is p. This twisted brown shape I see before me (S – the subject) is the shell of a hickory nut (P – the predicate). The universal concept of nut and the smaller archetype of the hickory has expanded into perceptual and individual sensible life through this one nutshell. I feel its texture with my hands. In judging, I link this twisted brown shape and its texture, size, profile, and weight with an idea that I do not externally see before me. I do not feel the texture of the <u>idea</u> of a nut with my hands. Now, if we set aside the contents of the percept (the color, shape, texture, size, profile, weight), I can follow the movements of the will in thinking as it is forming judgments and conclusions. Note that it is the individual perspective of the I of the earthly human which provides the link between the universal and the singular. We find that there is a realm in the sphere of judgment that is concerned wholly with the consistency, organization, and harmony of the world of propositions,

---

[82] *Goethe's World Conception*, chap 11

interpretations, and ideas. This power of thought investigates, orients, and draws inferences and connections within the pre-existent world of thinking and belief that dwells in the field of operative concepts that are open to an individual human being. This power that is concerned with consistency, with fitting each new judgment into the overall edifice of thoughts, stands at a transitional stage between the primary stage of hermeneutic attenuation (the blink of an eye where I recognize the sense of what I am thinking) and later phases of reckoning a judgment in terms of truth function. Husserl calls this *consequence-logic* or the *logic of non-contradiction*. Is there an innate spiritual harmony in the wholeness of world-thinking, as viewed from the cosmic perspective?

Steiner speaks of the fact that a lone, newly formed proposition or series of thoughts can never stand on its own, but is naturally absorbed and interrelated with the overall flexible structure of the spiritual substance that conceptualization molds. The Greater Logic of Hegel traces the nodes and details of this development using intellectual intuition in a theoretical way, without crossing the threshold. This is part of what Steiner means when he says, "The content of this thinking appears to us as an organism inwardly complete in itself; everything is in strictest interconnection. The individual parts of the thought-system determine each other; every single concept ultimately has its roots in the wholeness of our edifice of thoughts." Husserl wants to trace how this strict interconnection is accomplished. As we have seen, a partial extract of this thought edifice can be experienced in a preliminary way in its half dying projection around the area of the head. Moral and threshold work can further transform our consciousness of it, given favorable karma, into the pure concepts that are unveiled in moral intuition. A larger question could be – how are limited or partial truths incorporated into the wholeness of the world edifice of cosmic thought? We know that even materialism has its proper place in the rotation of worldviews, but where does the moral difference arise between a partial viewpoint of the whole truth and an outright lie, which produces destruction in the astral world?[83]

In his introductions to Goethe's scientific works, Steiner describes how each phenomenon is absorbed into the harmony of world thought: "When I approach it {an individual object}, it faces me as a single thing. Within me the thought-world presses toward that spot where the concept of the thing lies. I do not rest until that which confronted me at first as an individual thing appears as a part of my thought-world. Thus, the individual thing as such dissolves and appears in a larger context. Now it is illuminated by the other thought-masses; now it is a **serving member**; and it is completely clear to me what it signifies with the greater harmony. This is what takes place in us when we approach the object of experience and contemplate it. All progress in science depends upon our becoming

---

[83] I cannot follow the question further here. See Steiner, (GA 99), lecture 6, May 30, 1907

aware of the point at which some phenomenon or other can be incorporated into the harmony of the thought-world. Do not misunderstand me. This does not mean that every phenomenon must be explainable by concepts we already have, that our world of ideas is closed, nor that every new experience must coincide with some concept or other *that we already possess.* That pressing of the thought-world within us toward a concept can also go to a spot that has not yet been thought by anyone at all. And the ideal progress of the history of science rests precisely on the fact that thinking drives new configurations of ideas to the surface."[84]

We experience in a thinking-perception (that is, in direct participation with our capacity to see the unfoldings of thinking-flow in meaning- and form-landscapes which are not sensible), that a perception, a feeling, or an experience arises for which we do not yet have a concept. So, our willing-meaning-searcher, penetrates intuitively (with faster moving fire streams

---

[84] Steiner, Rudolf. *Goethean Science (GA 1),* translator, Lindemann, Mercury Press, Spring Valley, NY, 1988. p. 128. In the same section, Steiner also uses the Hegelian difference between *Verstand* (the intellectual understanding) and *Vernunft* (the dialectical flow of ideal reason) to explain the difference notions that individuals may hold about the same object. "The intellect *(Verstand)* creates thought-configurations for the individual things of reality. It fulfills its task best the more exactly it delimits these configurations, the sharper the contours are that it draws. Reason *(Vernunft)* then has to incorporate these configurations into the harmony of the whole world of ideas." p 129.

154

in larger clouds of warmth) into the folds of meaning-concept-light. It accomplishes its flight at infinite speed (as Deleuze points out) in every direction at once, and the will in meaning kneads an impression on the lit-up substance of concepts, bringing to birth a new idea. The paternal laser of the will impregnates the field of the mothers of new thoughts. The *prima materia* grows new sensation-light for the angels in the heavenly world. A new child is born in the spiritual world. This new idea is then merged into the dough of the infinite, flexible light and meaning-concept life, which flows invisibly together with our personal mind. In the etheric world, we find that such an idea is instantly multiplied and copied in a simultaneous reproduction and transmission of thinking seeds. The flowing streams and the copying process itself are intimately linked in the etheric world.

At the far side, the spirit that lies behind the concept connected with the specific judgment is in turn a 'serving member' of the whole spiritual world. We in our spiritualized thinking can also become a free actor in the world-harmony that renders a humble service to the whole of reality by returning our love to the miracle of knowledge. We warm the gift of wisdom we have received, by taking it into our human hearts. This means that what was given by the spiritual world as the firework that explodes in the precise second of understanding the meaning of something, is transformed and expanded as we give it back in love to the angelic world. This is one way in which Anthroposophia and Philosophia can join hands through the conscious human I, penetrated by

155

the Event of our times. We can then become serving members in the Michaelic mathesis universalis, which is cosmic intoned spirit logic.

But what can be thought? What is reasonable? What is irrational and unable to be mortised together in a cunning fashion? There seem to be at least three different aspects of the logic of non-contradiction:

1. There is the system of logical axioms which govern the interplay of a set of logical statements in an argument or syllogism. Husserl is right to point out that one may, even in setting up truth tables in the analysis of a particular set of arguments, focus entirely on whether the set of statements is consistent. One may evaluate the logical consistency of the series of statements, without the further logical analysis that focuses on the truth of the major premise. Indeed, many writers on logic consider a statement to be true if it conforms to the fundamental rules of inference, without reference to the validity of the content. But such a viewpoint only shows us how shallow our experience of truth is today. An argument may be logically consistent, but still false, if its fundamental propositions are false in regard to the actual state of affairs. One need only imagine the perfectly logical forms of thought that could be arranged to defend morally criminal acts.

2. In the operation of the spiritual aspect of the mind, an unconscious action organizes new propositions, sense-judgments, and concepts drawn from a variety of experiences, into the overall edifice

of the mind's conceptual sphere – without focusing on whether or not the new concept is necessarily true. It is rationally linked to relative ideas. The elements of larger organic sets are interwoven according to similarity of form and original similarity of resonance. This is the work of the spiritual world and its beings.

3. Welton, in *The Other Husserl*, focuses on a third aspect in his analysis of the transition from accepting reports to analyzing claims explicitly. It is possible to receive an intuitive report coming directly in the concept plane which one understands and accepts provisionally. Later, after it has connected with the whole of the thought world, I can consciously begin to investigate its network. Sometimes it becomes necessary to participate in the expansion of the essence of the concept which was intuitively received or 'reported' or, on the other hand, to re-orient some of the links.[85]

But if I consciously create the new links and incorporations into the pulsing, interwoven sets of organically living knowledge, this 'report' was not created by someone else, but was directly created through intuitive and novel thinking in the concept folds. At the end of myself, IT walks across great distances and tracts, like cosmic lands, to be created anew in world cosmic thinking. Then, if I remember my Self, and actualize the source of my freedom, the All can be brought near by the action of the self-intuiting I AM in understanding. Using the language

---

[85] See pp 191-193 in his excellent book

of Steiner's *Truth and Science* - in the act of cognition, I (who am part of the given, and use the powers given to me) create something new out of the given, when I transform its wholeness in thinking; simultaneously, both my subjectivity and the given are also conceptually formed and transformed.[86] When one receives a report or, what is the same, intuits a concept, it is possible to confront the idea while experiencing it. This means that even though it can be linked temporarily to the whole edifice of thought (the virtual encyclopedic fabric), I may later perform a calm and healing re-orientation and re-evaluation on it, reflecting on it, carefully uncovering its connections, and re-inserting it in a new configuration of connections. But everything is reabsorbed like light shining into more light. However, if I do not enact Steiner's powerful tool of 'confront while experience' in regard to receiving the report, then I end up unconsciously accepting its claims, and the concept begins to function by controlling all of the ramifications of experience and perception that are linked back to it, as the proto-model. Furthermore, the more extensively I consider these issues in a Husserlian fashion, the more I construct an edifice of dead thought sludge around the head. The astral body, which is required for consciousness, brings wakefulness into the streams of light required for personal thought in the ether body, but it also brings death, when the astral is connected to the ether during

---

[86] "It is essential to realize that the activity of producing something in the act of cognition must present itself to us as something also directly given." GA 3, p. 60

158

our hours of wakeful activity. In order to use the dying streams of old judgments as fertilizer to plant new seeds in the world of life, I could transform it using Ben-Aharon's technique from *The New Experience of the Supersensible*. Here, I separate the content from the force of the representations, and then pull the force down into the back of the head, and with love, slowly pour it into the heart, creating drop by drop the new etheric (or virtual) spirit-blood of human morality.[87] What was killed in the ether body can be brought to life again.

I may also resurrect what is dead in my thinking and my being through the shock of the other. When I am meeting another person and listening to her, I may also register the meaning of her thoughts without yet judging them as true or false. In an exercise of transforming thinking by following the other in me (or I in the other), one may perceive the substantive transformations, qualitative transpositions, and flight-patterns (so to speak) of a particular flow of human thinking. But this happens in the fluid emptiness of spirit light, where self-conscious Selves can socially and karmically breathe one another. As we found earlier, we are really swimming in the same thinking-ocean. But can we remember it spiritually and re-experience it now? These attempts at meeting will no doubt be mixed up in the clouds of all varieties of feeling, desire, motive, instinct, and sensation, but that is the human experience in its tragedy and richness.

---

[87] See pp 98-100 for the full Michaelic heart confrontation with what is dead in thinking

In such listening without sympathy or rejection, one attends to the propagations of the thought-forms as actual substances moving in a field of thought-perception rather than evaluating their noemata as either valid or invalid. We find more than we bargained for when we listen to another person in this way. This can be the source of new human communities, as we have found in our Global School and College work. As Levinas says, our hearts can be 'cored out' like an apple in these difficult meetings.[88] If I can experience the way that she breaks through all of my personal intentionality, I may find, on the yonder side, that she can give me part of my own self that I have forgotten. We help each other remember the soul and spirit parts that we forget at every second. But how is this experience woven into the planes of consistency without contradiction? At this moment, we may find all of the hidden fruit of the life of the virtual, where she and I become free of the old laws, but are grasped by the life of new possibilities. Yes, we are bound by spiritual law, since we are woven together with the spirits, but we also can create new life in a new day. This new revelation in thought is what Deleuze was trying to express in his search for something beyond bare contradiction and disjunction - his disjunctive syntheses and his vice-diction rose

---

[88] In *Otherwise than Being*. For details on this see my *Resurrection of Thinking*

from such an experience of living difference.[89] The future is born here.

Logic as a discovery of moral, karmic, and spiritual validity (*Geltung*) through the Christ Event

When we free ourselves from the mere image of thought, each decision is ultimately a spiritual and moral decision. This takes place every time I use my body, but also in each link, association or knotting that I perform using my combinatorial and synthetic powers on the proto-light blockchain (unlike a blockchain proper, however, the past states in the thought world are also changeable like an interweaving group of constellations that affect one another instantly and in the pure life of duration). In other words, there is a moral and spiritual will that fires up, when I create a movement and inference flow of human knowledge on the objective virtual encyclopedia-river. The states of affairs are ultimately spiritual beings and the relations between them, with their moral repercussions and karma, belong to the harmonic and rhythmic cycling of logical inspiration and expiration between earth and Heaven. The spirit of Truth, coming from stars and planets, guides us outward and inward on this great river, and as

---

[89] See my *Resurrection of Thinking*, as well as Deleuze's *Difference and Repetition* and *The Logic of Sense*

Bosanquet said, one can only discover more truth through the action of Truth itself. It is its own sphere of moral-self-referential growth and opening and moral-spiritual education of the human-earthly cosmic. Truth has its own land. The spirit of truth opens and elucidates the path to experience and knowing truth. I can open my heart to it. Each logical joining and knotting (the Husserlian process of *Verknüpfung*) is a deadening, but also it can be seen spiritually and full of soul from the outside, and in a new, totally contemporary and modern spiritual scientific and Michaelic technique, one can re-enliven this deadened knotting into an experience of spiritual co-working between Christ, man, angel and elemental spirits.[90]

Earthly and Heavenly logical validity are nourishing one another, in the midst of another simultaneous flow of affection, quality, and sensation – of, as Deleuze calls it in *What Is Philosophy?* endo- and exo-sensation. And if my sensation can be filled with an open and flexible devotion, one can experience the becoming of a moral cogency, with the Spirits of Wisdom and Harmony of Feeling (or Sensation). Sensation breathes in a cosmic respiration, devotion grows in new days, fields, and times of the supersensible, and one discovers that each thought is a spiritual being. The sword of the spiritual

---

[90] This is the true answer to Kant's valid question of 'how is synthetic apriori knowledge possible?' - Spirit life is woven together and blossoms forth into new creation, which is known and loved as it is born. Human cosmic knowledge walks forward.

Individuality must then become calmly but actively awake to differentiate what I create in thinking's spiritual wells, and what wants to think for me. For we see that our evil thoughts and lies populate the spiritual world with monsters. But the I-Am of the human is not a little ego but a giant earthly-cosmic process of becoming the Truth, and it is filled with openness on all sides. Spiritual Logic pulses through the heart's sensitive spiritual blood. Such a logic does not bypass the rigorous empirical demands of evidence and careful, unbiased reasoning, but it spiritualizes the activity of such work, so that the foundations and activity are themselves observable, and can be described through concepts and language. This is a transcendental empiricism if such words are useful at all. In any case, this demonstrates that a spiritual science can exist alongside, and complete natural science. Intuition only improves human knowledge.

Husserl points out what counts as evidence in the intuitive phenomenological experience of thinking: "the giving of things themselves are the acts of producing evident legitimacy or rightness; they are creative primal institutings of rightness, or truth as correctness."[91] 'Back to the things themselves!' Husserl cried, but then the things stood up in the first beginning (*prima institutio*).[92] The problem that we

---

[91] FTL p 159

[92] Recall the etymological root of in-stitution in the Latin '*stare*,' which means 'to stand;' this is certainly also connected with the German *Stiftung* that Husserl uses here.

must face with deep seriousness, is the transformation of this epistemological and cognitive problem into a fully moral and spiritual experience of an ongoing battle, drama, and reformation of the moment by moment process of human knowledge. The things give themselves in a spiritual and soul blossoming, yes, but we do not recognize how they die in us, in our personal mental images. We built our skin out of the 'dead things themselves' that we wanted to care for so faithfully! What is the solution to our dying knowledge? In our times, we have the great joy to discover that the spirit of the living Christ is beginning to freely and gently work with humans from his new appearance in the etheric world, or world of real life. As Ben-Aharon points out and lives through with intimate accuracy, this fully conscious human transformation of knowledge and life has three stages:

> The **first** impression received by Christ's illumination reveals the darkening death forces woven into man's life organism...In the **second** stage, self-knowledge changes into self-transformation. Man knows himself to be known by Christ, i.e. an active cognitive interrelationship is established, in which man no longer sees only himself (darkly) by means of Christ's light, but he knows himself as Christ knows him, that is, not through death but through resurrected, eternal life...This is where we find St Paul's second, most sacred ground of being: when the 'I' holds fast to true self-knowledge, seeing still only partly and darkly but knowing clearly what is the source of his partiality, namely, seeing without delusion his active, opaqueness-creating Death being...**(3)** Yet

this is not I, as Saul, but I in and through the consciousness-awakening Death being of Saul that became Paul at the gates of Damascus, who is a completely new being moulded according to Christ's likeness from the very roots of human existence. Saul-Paul in me is thus perfected as my unshakeable anchorage of freedom and love, consciously bridging the infinite abyss between the Son of God and the Son of Man, the first and the last Adam in me.[93]

We see there that knowing the truth about thinking, love, and activity as a complete human being living in the world, is not just a stroll through the grass, while remaining in ordinary consciousness, perceiving only the material world. Phenomenology could only become spiritual science if its darkness is first pierced through by the *photismos* of Christ's appearance. It requires a real spiritual scientific process of the construction of the threefold mirror of the etheric body as a whole, that was only brought to clarity and demonstrated by Rudolf Steiner's work and life. Epistemology cannot remain intellectual ponderings about logic or scientific principles. But this illumination can indeed come about through the practice of the living art of *The Philosophy of Freedom*. Knowledge itself is a life and death process, it is a rich soul process and battle, and it is a moral process that is linked to the spiritual world and its beings itself, since they are the root and reality of all knowledge processes. Experiencing the self-evidence of the truth happening does not mean that one just

[93] *The New Experience of the Supersensible*, p 38

gives up one's own personal capacity for thinking in order to participate in the sentimental feelings of religious emotion. This goes beyond the vague positions of the various catechisms. Anthroposophy can be demonstrated as a moral and cognitive path without using religious or spiritual terminology at all, as was shown in the construction of the spiritual art work that lives and functions behind the words of *The Philosophy of Freedom.* This anthroposophical drama and catastrophe and chaos of true knowledge happening in the 21st century and beyond must enter with even greater scientific and empirical strictness (but now honed and lifted into spiritual scientific accuracy and expansiveness and life) into the real events of the etheric, soul, and spiritual worlds to a degree that was never accomplished by any phenomenologist. Nor was it accomplished by Husserl's student, Edith Stein, nor theologians like Von Balthasar, or supposed 'anthroposophists' like Tomberg. Such people, who indeed possess many merits, developed their powerful insights in ways that were definitely not an outcome of spiritualizing thinking. However, a truly contemporary spiritual science that penetrates first into the dying forces of thinking, is not only possible but it is happening now, beyond the orthodox limits of all fraternities of the past, who are still working sensibly and supersensibly to prevent it. It is happening in the life behind this very book.

The new self-evidence that must come to full saturation, is the shocking fact that my consciousness is constructed through the luciferic and ahrimanic doubles who take up residence inside my earthly personality, and indeed who act as me a great deal of the time. This elevates the consciousness active in Husserl's work. We see this sobering self-knowledge expressed in art forms from the 19th century onwards, from Dostoyevsky's 'The Double', Wilde's *The Picture of Dorian Gray* and as recently as Peele's 2019 movie 'US'. It is the luciferic spirit especially that is often not recognized by people interested externally in anthroposophy and other new age pursuits, as well as in religious institutions. Christ's real nature is confused with Lucifer, and the real spiritual experience is replaced unconsciously with a different world altogether, where the human is definitely not free in his or her Individuality.[94] Lucifer gives the gift

---

[94] Steiner says (GA 207), "In the Lemurian epoch — the first that concerns us to-day — it was the Luciferic Beings who intervened in man's evolution, in opposition to the Powers who at that time were striving to help him forward. In the Atlantean epoch, the Spirits opposing the progressive Powers were the Spirits of "Ahriman" or "Mephistopheles". The Ahrimanic or Mephistophelean Spirits — to give the precise names — are those known in medieval times as the Spirits of "Satan" — who must not be confused with "Lucifer". In our own epoch, as time goes on, other spiritual Beings of whom we shall speak later, will stand as hindrances in the path of the progressive Spirits. We will ask ourselves now: What did the Luciferic Spirits actually achieve in the ancient Lemurian epoch? These things will be considered to-day from a particular point of view. Of what domain did the Luciferic Spirits lay hold during the Lemurian epoch? The best way to understand this is to cast our minds back over the course taken by human evolution.

You know that on Old Saturn the Thrones poured out their own substance to lay the first foundation of the human

physical body. On Old Sun the Spirits of Wisdom imbued man with the ether- or life-body. And on the Earth the Spirits of Form endowed him with the 'I', the ego, in order that by realizing himself as distinct from his environment he might become an independent being. But even if through the deed of the Spirits of Form he had become independent vis-à-vis the external world surrounding him on earth, he would never have become independent of the Spirits of Form themselves; he would have remained dependent on them, he would have been directed by them as on leading-strings. That this did not happen was due to something which had, in a certain sense, a beneficial effect, namely the fact that in the Lemurian epoch the Luciferic Beings set themselves in opposition to the Spirits of Form. It was these Luciferic Beings who gave man the prospect of freedom — but therewith the possibility of evil-doing, of succumbing to passion and desire in the world of sense. Where did these Luciferic Beings actually take hold? They took hold of what had been instilled into man as his innermost member at that time — the astral body. They established their footing in the human astral body and took possession of it. Had it not been for the coming of the Luciferic Beings this astral body would have remained in the sole possession of the Spirits of Form. They would have instilled into this astral body the forces which give man his human countenance, making him into an image of the Gods, namely, of the Spirits of Form. All this man would have come to be; but in his life through all eternity he would have remained dependent upon the Spirits of Form.

The Luciferic Beings had crept, as it were, into man's astral body, so that Beings of two kinds were now working in it: the Beings who bring man forward and the Beings who, while obstructing this constant impulse, had at the same time established the foundations of his independence. Had the luciferic Beings not approached, man would have remained in a state of innocence and purity in his astral body. No passions inciting him to crave for what is to be found only on earth would have arisen in him. The

168

of speedy 'spiritual growth' by jumping past careful objective thinking, painful self-knowledge, and years of moral development. The primal acts of setting up rightness and truth inside one's own soul, standing up and grasping them in living concepts in a direct living thinking experience of their ultimate significance,

---

passions, urges and desires of man were densified, debased, as it were, by the Luciferic Beings. Had they not approached, man would have retained a perpetual longing for his heavenly home, for the realms of spirit whence he has descended. He would have taken no delight in what surrounds him on the earth; earthly impressions would have aroused no interest in him. It was through the Luciferic Spirits that he came to have this interest, to crave for the impressions of the earth. These Spirits impelled him into the earthly sphere by pervading his innermost member, his astral body. Why, then, was it that man did not fall away entirely at that time from the Spirits of Form or from the higher spiritual realms as a whole? Why was it that in his interests and desires he did not succumb wholly to the world of sense? It was because the Spirits who lead humanity forward took counter measures; they inculcated into the being of man what would otherwise not have been his lot, namely, illness, suffering and pain. That was the necessary counterweight to the deeds of the Luciferic Spirits. The Luciferic Spirits gave man material desires; as their countermeasures the higher Beings introduced illness and suffering as the consequences of material desires and interests, to the end that he should not utterly succumb to this world of sense. And so there is exactly as much suffering and pain in the world as there is interest only in the physical and the material. The scales are held in perfect balance; the one does not outweigh the other — so many passions and desires on the one side, so much illness and pain on the other. This was the effect of the mutual activities of the Luciferic Spirits and the Spirits of Form in the Lemurian epoch."

means to penetrate at least to the moral activity of the free I-AM who directs thinking activity. But the great I-AM sets up goodness inside of me. Understanding the meaning of categories like Position, Quality, and Goodness and perceiving their archetypal reality that weaves in spirit and life in the supersensible, already means in our times that we have to craft with the help of Michael, Christ, and the spiritual being of Anthroposophy. They bring both the real and the irreal epistemological moral insight, where the light of interior thinking and self-love becomes world rays of spirit light. Here I can recognize the temptations of the excessive poles of Lucifer and Ahriman working in me. But the two poles must be there, so that I can find the middle, as in Harris' illustration for the 2nd degree tracing board reprinted earlier in the book. In Tolkien's terminology, neither the tower of Orthanc nor Barad-Dur lead to the true path of goodness, which requires both the humility of the hobbits and the death and transformation of Mithrandir. In the masonic path, I must be killed and wakened from death in the third degree to see through the illusions of the grid which were discovered in the second degree. Spiritual scientific phenomenology must mean spiritual battles, devotion, and self-recognition. 21st century epistemology must now mean conscious co-working with spiritual beings and other human beings in a new creative way in full freedom and in growing love and helping.

If we wish to invite Husserl and Fichte to the altar of the human side of the Michael School that Rudolf Steiner has now created in the supersensible world, it must mean that all of the self-creative light of opening thinking must now be laid on the burning fire of the altar of the heart. The spirits behold transcendental idealism coming to life in men's souls. But this sacrifice does not either put out the fire, or diminish the light. It rather allows for the hardened crystals of the quartz and silicon carved by the phenomenological and idealist forefathers in the world-memory to melt and become fructified by the spirit of the seed of Anthroposophia. Then it becomes world-wide Christ light. But all of this is the most uplifting and inspiring story, because it shows us that all human activity, science, art, knowledge creation, and community formation can be nourished by the Spirit of the Earth, who is the soul of the Earth. Yes, we must look maturely into the fact that each human crucifies and kills the spirit by using the 'conscious organ of sin' of his being of death in his head to kill the Spirit of Christ at every moment. But once this is seen, and I remain awake to my personal capacity for evil, we can help one another to begin to build a new type of human, spread out in life-fields over the whole earth, transferring gifts of knowledge, love, and economic resources to each culture, family, and person as they need it; all penetrated by spiritualized heart's blood, karmic will fire, and starry filled gentle thinking. This wakefulness of Christ's intensifying spiritual impulse of Freedom in the 21st century and beyond far into the future, is the spiritual-logical 'sum of conditions' (Hobbes and Mill) that exist as a potential spark that can light the fire for humans. But the sum of conditions or the supersensible spark is not enough by itself to be the cause of transformation, rather the initiative of free humans must consciously build this bridge for real manifestation to take place. This is one path in which earthly and transcendental logic can be transformed into spiritual moral logic through the Event of our time.

Chapter 8 – Into the Unconscious: Devotion and Active Forgetting as Preparation for Inspiration

How do we exist in the stream of time? What is the container of our sense life and why doesn't it ever become full? How do we remember past experiences at all? Where do we look when we gaze at a memory image? What arm do we use to wipe away the memory image from our mind's eye? How are our feelings and emotions attached to memories of the past? How do we forget something in the present that we remembered in the past? How is our own personal life connected to the surging flow of the ocean-like world all around us? These are questions that curious people have always struggled to understand. Philosophical inquiry and scientific research have tried to solve these riddles for centuries. Husserl himself uncovered immensely complex enigmas of consciousness as he delved into the full and rich life of the soul as a whole. He attempted to fully comprehend the barely detectable changes in the tangled layers of perception, attentiveness, remembering, forgetting, and anticipation as they swarm together in the flow of each moment. If we described his activity in anthroposophical language, he demonstrates that he is a fully modern human insofar as he progresses more and more deeply into the use of the faculties of the consciousness-soul. Here he considers the perception of a table:

> Every perception, or noematically speaking, every single aspect of the object in itself, points to a continuity, to multifarious continua of possible new perceptions, and precisely to those in which the same object would show itself from ever new sides...What is identical is a constant x, a constant substrate of actually appearing table-moments, but also of indications of moments not yet appearing...They are, however, not single indications, but entire indicative systems, indications functioning as systems of rays that point toward corresponding manifold systems of appearances. They are pointers into an emptiness...Everything that genuinely appears is an appearing thing only by virtue of being surrounded by a halo of emptiness with respect to appearance. It is an emptiness that is not a nothingness, but an emptiness to be filled-out; it is a determinable indeterminacy...What is only co-present entails a distinction between determinations with respect to the content of the object [a] that are actually there, appearing in the flesh, and [b] those that are still ambiguously prefigured in full emptiness.[95]

Let us carefully separate the layers of consciousness, perception, willing, and thinking that Husserl notices. When Husserl mentions 'rays' he is usually discussing the motion of the will that is operational in attention from moment to moment. These are the thin arms that work in the willing (and

---

[95] APAS pp 41-43

feeling) part of the soul which make it possible for our normal subjective thinking to locate, organize, connect, and reflect elements of understanding and form, back into the mental image space inside and around the head. They are crystallizing tentacles that work in a solidifying and condensing manner. These permit the reversing and paralyzing activity of the creation of mental images and representations to occur. They are like an oxidizing or deadening element inside our head consciousness that we have dealt with in detail earlier. In this way, I orient the mental image as part of the process to understand that what I am seeing is, for example, one side of a rainbow-colored kite flying in the blue sky. Yet, in this passage, Husserl starts to become aware that these webs of feeling and will that are oriented toward future possible profiles of the object, unfold with a sort of automatic and anonymous anticipation. The machine in us, filled with the desire to know and possess by representing in its little cave, rattles on. He also notices the boundaries of the operation, where the signs and tentacles of intention point into the halo of emptiness. They reach the unexplorable.

In addition, Husserl discusses the noematic realm, where the essence or conceptually vibrant meaning of what I am perceiving and thinking about, is revealed to thinking's direct grasp. In this region, I intuit the concept of any kite whatsoever, and indeed every possible appearance of this particular kite from every side. The purely conceptual meaning of any kite whatsoever is thought from the interior of the concept, in full saturation, while there is also a secondary ray

of attention that is involved in the living rotation of
the various sides of this particular kite in the space of
mental images. If this rotation is kept alive in
imaginative variation, then the particular profiles are
not actually seen in the mental image sphere, but
rather the potential for these possible appearances is
meaningfully evident as a virtual seed flux. It is of
course also possible to view the profiles themselves in
the mind's eye, but this takes place in a third region of
attention. Another region of attention rises up from
the depths of a 'full emptiness.'[96]

---

[96] Actually, the complete picture of what happens in
perception, representing, and moving the attention is quite
complex. We have:

1. Pure percept in normal consciousness (Husserl's hyle)
2. Word strings in intellectual soul (represented)
3. Inner gestures of possible speech prefigured in larynx
   region (representational or subjective level)
4. Mental image (barely consciously written on light grid of
   intellectual soul and dying etheric light)
5. Noematic Core after variation, appearing only in head
   region & Eidos (still subjective)
6. Goethean Archetype revealing itself, after noematic core is
   brought into the heart (on the threshold)
7. Representations of tactile features and weight of object that
   are operative in sensation, feeling, and willing parts of the
   soul.
8. Full emptiness, coming from vague feeling of the other side
   of the threshold
9. The Real concept itself, perceived in moral intuition (middle
   zone)
10. Spiritualized percept, where the etheric body flows into the
    world ether (other side of threshold)

This is the most important element in Husserl's description, which opens one doorway into a soul-filled and spiritual enlivening of his phenomenology from the anthroposophical perspective. What is 'ambiguously prefigured in full emptiness?' This can provide a window into an element of the real soul experience that Husserl was never able to perceive with full insight from both inside and outside its living activity. Can we dive into this rolling, warm, flowing emptiness that is full of anticipation and endless transformation and development? Can we swim down into what is about to become a figure, or an image, rising out of the vague depths of what is coming toward us? How do we do this?

In Steiner's *Riddles of the Soul* (GA 21), we find a potent spark that can ignite our whole spiritualization of Husserl's problems into a gentle careful blaze. He shows us a very subtle difference between two aspects of the soul that work in forming mental images or memory images.[97] It took me years to finally

---

11. Etheric cognition of Imaginative elements of object as real being(s) in the Etheric world.

[97] "Just as a study of the nutritive value of seeds addressed something different than the developmental laws of plant growth, so an epistemology that investigates how the cognitive power of mental pictures reproduces reality, informs us about something different than the essential nature of our life of mental picturing. Just as little as it lies prefigured in the essential nature of a seed to become food, does it lie in the essential nature of mental picture to provide cognitive reproductions of reality...The truth is that in its mental pictures, the soul grasps its own evolving

experience this difference and to fully understand what he was really talking about. The best part about this new research is that we can use everything that is truly helpful from Husserl's intense investigations as wonderful fuel to continue to elevate our human consciousness. We do not have to somehow just ignore everything that Husserl accomplished and to return to Brentano or Lotze. Husserl's work can be resurrected from the dead, enlivened and moulded, intensified from the outside, from the real soul and spiritual worlds. This shows us why Steiner always advised us to return to the study of books written in the past – we can help bring the living spirit beings of the thoughts contained in them, one step further in their evolution, through new human and cosmic thinking cooperation. Our creative thinking adds new life to the universe.

This important distinction in the powers of the soul that work in mental picturing can be understood by the analogy of the difference between [a] the nutritive element present in a seed and [b] its reproductive aspect that can repeat its form and grow in the future. It is much easier to understand and view the first aspect of the mental image and not the second transitional element. I nourish my normal subjective power of thinking, by forming mental pictures in the first place. For example, I can perceive as a memory image the face and body of my grandma looking out

---

being. And only through the soul's own activity does it occur that mental pictures become the mediators of any knowledge and reality." *Riddles of the Soul* pp 17-18

her kitchen window. We can see then through the moral self-knowledge that comes from spiritual science, how this subjective head-centered representation-juggling, is an ahrimanic and luciferic creation that is glued together and which provides a basis for our contemporary self-consciousness. All of this can be accompanied by the moral shock of the reversal which is so clearly described by Yeshayahu Ben-Aharon in *Spiritual Science in the 21st Century*.

But in addition to this nutritive (dying) element, I can also carefully and gently develop my love and devotion to a higher and deeper degree and approach the same memory picture of my grandma again. If I can pour out enough love and devotion, based not on fantasy and deception, but based on real progress from transforming my habits, deeds, and my life as a whole, then I can carefully and gently unhusk the mental image or memory image, and pay attention to the pregnant pool of filled and warm emptiness all around the image, and in my whole soul flowing around me and together with the environment. Through this careful, humble, and gentle dissecting or pealing of the mental image, I can gracefully and joyously begin to actively repress the image parts of the representation and the memory. I can actively but gently forget the actual picture qualities and any of the light flux left over from any imaginative variation that I may have performed. If we follow the wholeness of this pregnant warmth, we can find that it is not just my head that is interested in remembering, but that the powers that form thinking and the soul's feelings, willing, and transformation are flowing all around the whole body,

179

head to toe and far outside the body. My pregnant warmth and anticipatory emptiness is flowing out in a world-pulse all around. I can follow the inner development of my soul to a place where I can then patiently wait for the grace of the living spiritual worlds to reveal themselves or sound themselves or express themselves in this threshold space. This part is not up to my subjectivity or my desires. The same process can be repeated with an audio memory, or a song fragment. This is more difficult than repressing and forgetting and following the visual image memory, but is also very fruitful. It takes a good deal of practice. Such an anthroposophical procedure accomplished with tone can extend Husserl's preliminary work outlined in *The Phenomenology of Internal Time-Consciousness.*

That is the wonderful part about human memories, that their seeds can continue to grow, even though we may have devoured and reversed the real world in the first moment that we created them originally. In this way, Husserl's dead crystalline structures become wonderful nourishment for the whole spiritual world today, if we can enliven them and offer them up, after having melted them and deposited them as fertilizer inside my own newly born human soul, life, thinking, and consciousness. Through these acts, taught to us by the risen Christ, we watch in joy as humans dance on their own graves, seeing their ancient work spring to new life, and the work of their whole lives, sprouting new opportunities for the growth of love, community, culture, and invention. Also, through these acts of new research,

180

one repays the debts to former teachers – I show thanks to all of the clarity that Husserl taught to me by dedicating myself to a spiritual rebirthing of his work, and all the more so for Rudolf Steiner's vast corpus, which reading in normal consciousness has turned into a corpse.

Steiner elaborates and demonstrates the very subtle fact that when the etheric image power dies it gives the direct support to the inner life of human mental picturing. But it is only when one can trace what does not die in the life of the mental image forming power, that one can see the pulse and life of the soul and etheric body's life itself. This can then sustain a new type of consciousness, which, if perceived by the spiritual I, living in the midst of spiritualized concepts, can morally view this process a bit from the outside.   This is a new life of consciousness, which is not formed by the dampening down to the point of paralysis which underlies the stability of our subjective consciousness and thinking. It can now flow in warmth in the soul, in a new light in the life body, in new silent tones, and spiritualized I-consciousness flowing through the whole world, before the division between inner and outer arises. This is of course beyond Husserl's eidetic images as well as Goethe's archetypal forms. This is the place where spiritual scientific consciousness arises, which has nothing to do with the subjective pictures inside the mind's eye. This basic fact that underlies the whole of Anthroposophy from Steiner's first work is usually totally misunderstood or not experienced, unfortunately.

But if we can truly penetrate, understand, and experience what Steiner means by the following words, then we can reach the living spirit of Anthroposophy once again:

> With the power of love, the exercises in forgetting can be practiced with greater force, and the results will be surer, than without it. By practicing self-discipline, which gives us a greater capacity for love, we are able to experience an enhanced faculty of forgetting, which is just as surely a part of our willing as is the enhanced faculty of remembering. We gain the ability to put something definite, something of a positive soul content, in the place of what is normally at the end of experience. Normally when we forget something, this marks the end of some sequence of experiences. Thus, in place of what would normally be nothing, we are able to put something positive. In the enhanced power of forgetting, we develop actively what otherwise runs its course passively. When we have come this far, it is as if we had crossed an abyss within ourselves and reached a region of experience through which a new existence flows toward us...These images fill with something coming from the other side of life, so to say. They fill with spiritual reality...This flowing of spiritual reality into the depth of our soul, this is what in my book *Knowledge of the Higher Worlds and Its Attainment*, I have called 'Inspiration.'[98]

Let us now connect this technique with the research of Husserl into the diminishing registration of content that occurs in forgetting and the dynamic alteration of amplitude of concentration in the normal

---

[98] *Anthroposophy and Science*, GA 324, 1921 p 72

flow of attentiveness and observation. What can come to life and awaken in us, when we willfully and lovingly fall asleep into forgetfulness? Can the colorless breath of the Other wake us?

Research into Spheres of Attentiveness outside the Centrality of Local Reflection. Following Husserl into a Phenomenology of the Unconsciousness and Forgetfulness.

Can we stay awake while falling asleep? Can we consciously watch the erasing that takes place in forgetting? Can we remain awake outside our little reflective light-closet? In his analysis of how unities of sense are formed, maintained for a while and then diminished as the central focus of attention flows elsewhere, Husserl says the following:

> If a datum that has just begun is awakened, the awakening will continue to proceed further; the awakening accompanies the datum that is continually unfolding, but will lose the datum in this unfolding, for example, through a diminution of intensity, through the effacement of contours and the like with respect to affectively significant conditions...the continual transference of affective force will exercise a steady awakening upon what is less favorable, consequently working against the affective diminution, halting it...Are there not regulated inhibiting, weakening counter potencies

183

which, by not letting affection arise any longer, also make the emergence of self-subsistent unities impossible, unities in other words that would not emerge at all with affection? These questions are difficult to answer...especially if we wish to make our way from the sphere of the living present into the sphere of forgetfulness and to comprehend reproductive awakening... Thus, our considerations concern a phenomenology of the so-called unconscious.[99]

Let us use an example to help understand him. First, I observe the leaves of a *Syngonium* plant and then enter into the reduction and only attend to the noema of the leaves, which means keeping half of a mental eye open to the essential meaning of the whole plant in the background. If I wish to reproduce the sense impression of the heart-shaped leaves in a clear mental image, I find that there are certain resistances on the fabric of imagination that produce obscurity on one side or another. It is especially difficult to reproduce the bright intensity of certain colors in the mind's eye. This is no problem with the Syngonium itself, since the green leaf is not particularly bright. But as I try to use my power of 'affective force' to reawaken the sides of the leaf that I cannot quite reproduce in the mind's eye, I find that I already 'know' what I am trying to form, even if I can't form it. This demonstrates the continual background potency of the morphological aspect of the category in the meaning realm beyond.

---

[99] APAS, pp 200-201

But Husserl is recognizing that even as I try to recreate mental images of 5 of the leaves as seen in external perception, I do not possess complete control over the layers of attention, meaning-orientation, imaginative painting capacities, memory clarity, and understanding which takes place in my soul and mind. There are multiple clouds of allure, temporary loss of focus, forgetfulness followed by 'taking another go at it,' other motivations to become distracted which do not seem to come from my own personality. There are multiple layers of twisting clouds of desire, straight rays of linear organization, colored layers of watery feelings, smoky hints, magnetic yearnings, brightness of wakefulness sailing above it all, and so on. This happens at every minute in my soul and mind. This is the normal realm of sensitive consciousness. But all of this weather of meaningful understanding and emotional currents, all of these clouds that become brighter or become heavier and darker by the minute, all revolve around a rising solid mountain or tall tree of unity in the centralizing organ systems of the body (now we are looking at the whole situation from a little outside this organization, following it into the realms of unconsciousness).

If we continue to pluck fruit from Husserl's path and then deepen it with Imaginative Cognition by stepping outside our inner soul bubble, to see it a bit more from the outside, we find the following. There is what could be called an inner soul lake in the middle of the body, it is made of a reflective light and watery, flexible substance. What is present at this particular moment to the normal mode of pressure of our attentive, affection, and emotions at time T, is constructed inwardly gathered and intensified in a minor way in the center of this inner soul pool. What I am presently conscious of in normal consciousness is what is contained and held in this pool of inwardly intensified light.

The unity of the present meaning of what we are perceiving, feeling, sensing, or thinking about representationally is woven and coalesced in this pool of chest and belly light. Certainly, there are the dead fluctuations in the head of more linear and propositional representational associations and linguistic constructions, but at the same time, there is a richer and brighter lake below, where I feel myself to be a self as a unity. Simultaneously, what I am presently focused on is reflected – as if there were walls of small mirrors on all sides of this lake which then reflect the concern or the present unity of affection and attraction and attention (note the 'a' in all of these words just used indicates the reaching out and pulling of the external elements outside my subjectivity into this lake; this same element produces the difference in Husserl between ap-perception and perception).

If we wish to follow the technique of Steiner in regard to the Syngonium, we consciously now unclothe and erase all of the mental images, and withhold our concentration toward its normal meaning and sense. We also repress the normal concepts of nature, plant, body, etc. We gently pour out our love and devotion to the unknown, in the

186

emptiness. We can indeed carefully erase the clouds and the weather inside the soul, and can indeed to a certain degree 'erase' the mountain, the upright tree, or the body itself. This allows us to view the inner logic of the various organs and elements of the body from a different side. We recognize the unifying function of the heart and its tendency toward coordinating things into wholeness. We note then the syllogism of the soul and spiritual body which lives inside our mineral body. We have all of the logical, syntactical and grammatical elements in our body itself - the linear and the oblique, symmetrical development, reproduction of the same, unity, motion of inference in the flow of blood and lymph to the extremities, causality in the muscles and disjunction in the joints of our limbs. These are all concepts which grow spiritually in the interior of the body. The human body is a shrunken cosmic syllogism. Causality is not a concept that arises from pure perception. Rather the notion of causality and connectivity is implied or essentially and spiritually pulsing in the growth of our mineral body itself, as well as in the will-components that allow our body to move, grasp things, step on the earth, etc. The inner body is a group of living and pulsing ideas, which give rise to concepts of thought on one side, and which give rise to organic forms in which we live and breathe, run and jump, love and storm on the other. The 7 forms of the main logic gates are derived from the same forces that produce the 7 openings in the skull, for example.

Would it go too far to say that beneath this luciferic lake of inwardness, we can await for the lady

187

of the lake to come to us, bringing inspiration from the depths of the other side (in this case, below the enigma of the diaphragm that Ben-Aharon discusses in *Cognitive Yoga*), in the form of a spiritual lightning sword? Can we freely take up this sword as a differentiating I-organ that is awake in all places, or as many places as the grace of the Logos and the Christ spirit allow? The Lady below the lake is one of the mothers, carrying the secret of the Other, of the formless emptiness of Spirit, and of the sub-earthly lightning. Then all three Mothers could arrive, bringing the hot wire, the neutral wire, and the ground wire, but all of this coordinated by a heart that reaches down, pouring its blood into the three tongues of fire arising from the will of God – in the Good, the Beauty, and the Truth. We could see a path to re-deeming the old evil living at the heart of electricity in this moment. We pull the fallen light from beneath the ground and return it to the shepherd of cosmic thought. This is how we will redeem the humans who have merged completely with computers in the future. But Ahriman is waiting there, to grasp the cord, when we fall asleep again.

Violet Wedge (1919), Kandinsky

Chapter 9 – Inference and Consequence: Logical Laws and Spiritual Laws

Lotze and the Problems of Logic

Inference is the mostly unconscious flow of a series of concepts on the virtual encyclopedia-flux down into a particular channel. It is usually performed in accordance with pre-arranged habits, which can be more or less rational. But when the spiritual researcher views the concept plane directly, it is seen that as one becomes conscious of this systematic supersensible hyper-fold or organic light-multiplicity, this ocean of human knowledge, one can now stop the natural 'gravity' of the liquid flow of inferring. I can now penetrate into the soul and spiritual sense of the concepts, to find new hidden elements which intersect from the back or the yonder. A window opens in the yonder, from the realms of the formless Spirit, which now interpenetrates the inference fields with a silent breath.

Judgment is then the conscious solidification and willful holding of a particular local region of the virtual-blockchain into a rigid form, which can then be used as a temporary ground to build the next link in the thinking process. Inference is a flow; judgment is a solidification, but performed by spiritual warmth, coordinating itself into the living organ system of the human spirit-body.[100]

---

[100] Steiner, GA 205, <146 -148> "When we wake up from a dream, we perceive especially strongly this weight down there of chaotic, illogical swirls of images, and we can notice how we see the will, which then arranges what lives there in us in such a way that it is logically ordered, striking into this chaotic swirl of images. But we don't take with us the logic of the world, which I previously called illogical, we only take with us the will. How is it that this will has a logical effect on us after all? You see, there is an important human secret here, something extremely important. It is this: When we immerse ourselves in cosmic existence, which does not exist for ordinary consciousness, when we immerse ourselves in our whole organization, then we feel in our will, which spreads out there, the cosmic logic of our organs. We feel the cosmic logic of our organs. It is extremely important to realize that when we wake up in the morning, that is, when we immerse ourselves in our body, we are forced by this immersion to form the will in a certain way. If our body were not already formed in a certain way, the will, would spin like a jellyfish on all sides when waking up; the will could strive chaotically like a jellyfish on all sides when waking up. It does not, because it dives into the existing human form. He dives into it, takes on all these forms; that gives him the logical structure. That's why he gives logic from the human body to the otherwise chaotically confused thoughts. At night, when man is asleep, he is gripped in the super-logic of the cosmos. He cannot hold on to it. But when he now dives into the body, the will takes on the form of the body. Just as if you were to pour water into a vessel and the water would if the will assumes the shape of the vessel, the will assumes the shape of the body. But not only, as when you pour water into a vessel and the water takes on the whole form of the vessel, it is not only so with the will that it takes on the spatial forms, but it flows into the smallest veins everywhere...In

191

humans, this will is divided into all the individual branches and from there it dominates the other chaotic flow of images. So that which one perceives as an undercurrent is, I would say, released from the body. It is also really released from the body, it is something that is connected to the human body, but which actually strives to continually free itself from the human body, which continually wants to come out of the forms of this human body. But that which a person carries out of his body when he falls asleep, that which he carries into the cosmos, that which then submerges, is in accordance with the law of the body. Now it is the case that with all the organization that is man's head organization, man would only come to images. It's a general physiological prejudice that we judge and form conclusions with the head, for example. No, we represent with the head. If we only had the head and the rest of the body was inactive for our life of forming mental representations, then we would be waking dreamers. For the head has only the ability to dream while awake. And when we return to our body in the morning, insofar as we pass through the head, the dreams come to our consciousness. Only when we penetrate deeper into our body again, when the will again adapts itself not only to the head, but to the rest of the organization, only then is this will again able to bring logic into the otherwise pictorially intertwining forces of images. This will then lead you to something that I have already presented in the past lectures. You have to be aware that man represents with his head and that in reality he judges, as strange and paradoxical as it sounds, with his legs and also with his hands, and then again forms conclusions with his legs and hands. This is how what we call a conclusion, a judgment, comes into being. When we form mental images, it is only the image that is radiated back into the head, but we make judgments and conclusions as a whole person, not just as a head person." DeepL translator and wordreference.com dictionaries are fantastic tools that are now available to scholars everywhere. Thanks to their developers.

Lotze in his *Logic in Three Books*, makes a wonderful statement about the flow of the logical process: "To develop the various forms of judgment systematically as members of a serious of operations, each of which leaves a part of its problem unmastered and thereby gives rise to the next."[101] The concept formations behind this statement, if discovered in clear sight and flexibility in their operation on the supple light substance of the living encyclopedia, retain a wonderful openness. We find a holistic triple movement here, which simultaneously arises as we think through issues - 1) We perceive the mental images that appear in the memory substance; 2) the formless concept-distances awaken and appear-in-meaning behind and throughout the lit-up substances, like dark ships in the night, world-large but so quiet, carrying meaning cargo. 3) We can move with spirit-warmth and balance down into the lower parts of the body, and find there the furnace and the walker of logical inference. I sit upon conclusions. My hand drops to rest upon the firmness. The moral warmth of the logical body walks its way through the cosmic spirit balance, carrying itself through time and living knowledge life.[102]

---

[101] P 44

[102] The Latin, *fero, ferre, tuli, latus,* from which we get inference, sublation, and modus tollens, means 'to carry'. I carry my body with the thinking I, walking it from the inside and outside, by in-ference. I stroll in the savoir-faire of conferring in human-logic sublation.

Every gesture of knowledge-creation and thinking changes the whole flexible substance and the constellations of what is lit-up and what is dark on the planes of concepts. This motion immediately leaves seeds in its wake, that can both grow on their own or inspire new thinkers that run into them. Anyone may also return to them later for contemplation or consideration of the same issue in future times. Each closing is a simultaneous opening – or each time the combine cuts a stalk, a new seed is planted behind it, and one need not wait until the spring for planting in logical thinking. There may indeed be a prime season for thinking-seed-plantings in the living encyclopedia, but nevertheless the movement of inference itself can leave potent proto-growths in its wake. My whole body of warmth, air, and gravity bears the children of nature in my bosom, like a mother of spirit knowledge. Each logo-eurythmic gesture of my body as a whole, leaves its trace as knowledge form in the pulsing streams of nature's unfolding roots. Thinking lives inside nature's wholeness. But as Steiner reminds us, the thinking must also live in the blood pulsing through my bodies.[103] And the body can take another

---

[103] GA 217, "Thoughts, however, must not be so feeble that they stick up there in the head. They must be so strong that they stream down through the heart and through the whole being of man, right down to the feet. For really it is better if, besides red and white blood corpuscles, thoughts, too, pulse through our blood. It is a good thing, certainly, when a man has a heart too, and not merely thoughts. Best of all is for thoughts to have a heart. And that has been lost altogether. We cannot cast off the thoughts that have followed in the wake of the last four or five centuries. But these thoughts must get a heart as well!"

194

step. Logic is the dancing apocalyptic book of nature becoming self-conscious.

But let us also note the whole growth of a nearby and interpenetrating field of virtue, goodness, beauty, and humble morality which can interact with the best plantings of spiritualized thinking. Here we find the new regions of human virtuous moral creative-thinking, where we can grow what is thought on the earth into a gift that is handed over to the spiritual hierarchies directly. This handing over, the spiritual form of modus tollens, lifting up what has been created here, is a self-conscious merging together without losing independence. The virtual encyclopedia (the spiritual brain) is a rather neutral ground morally, but it can be used in its best spiritual and human operations to weave it with the spiritual-blood and humble sacred grounds of creative altar building.[104] In this work, we build no earthly temples,

---

[104] To clarify the relationship between the human brain and the proto-light of the virtual blockchain one can look at Steiner's GA 204, lecture 2: "The fact is that in its plastic configuration the human brain is indeed an extraordinarily faithful replica of what we know as the life of thought. In the plastic configuration of the human brain, the life of thought really does express itself, we might almost say, in an adequate manner. In order to follow this thought to its conclusion, however, something else is needed. What ordinary psychology and also Herbart's psychology designate as chains of thoughts, as thought associations in the form of judgments, logical conclusions and so on, should not remain a mere idea. At least in our imagination — even if we cannot rise to clairvoyant Imaginations — we should allow it to culminate in a picture; the tapestry of

195

logic, the tapestry presented to us by psychology of the life
of thought, the teaching of the soul life, should be allowed
to culminate in a picture. If we are in fact able to transform
logic and psychology in a picture-like, plastic way into an
image, then the human configuration of the brain will
emerge. Then we shall have traced a picture, the realization
of which is the human brain...It is based on the fact that the
human brain, indeed the whole system of nerves and
senses, is a replica of an Imaginative element. We
completely grasp the wonderful structure of the human
brain only when we learn to investigate Imaginatively.
Then, the human brain appears as a realized human
Imagination. Imaginative perception teaches us to become
familiar with the external brain, the brain we come to know
through psychology and anatomy, as a realized
Imagination. This is significant. Another fact is no less
important. Let us bear in mind that the human brain is an
actual human Imagination. We are indeed born with a
brain, if not a fully developed one, at least with a brain
containing the tendencies of growth. It tries to develop to
the point of being a realized Imaginative world, to be the
impression of an Imaginative world. This is, as it were, the
ready-made aspect of our brain, namely, that it is the
replica of an Imaginative world. Into this impression of the
Imaginative world we then build the conceptual
experiences attained during the time between birth and
death. During this period we have conceptual experiences;
we conceive, we transform the sense perceptions into
thoughts; we judge, we conclude, and so on. We fit this into
our brain. What kind of activity is this? As long as we live
in immediate perception...the external world lives on in us
by penetrating our organism through the senses as through
channels. With our inner life, we encompass this external
world. But the moment we cease to have this immediate
experience of the outer world...this concreteness — our
interplay with the external world in perceiving —
penetrates into the depths of our soul. It may then be drawn
to the surface again in the form of pictures by memory. We

but give our harvests to the Michaelic spirits. Of course, we can bring new forms down into earthly farms and fridges too.

Let us take a concrete example. I infer that if the Japanese Maple branch grows any further it will be strangled by the rising tendrils of the Asiatic

---

may say that during our life between birth and death insofar as our thought life is concerned, our interplay with the external world consists of two parts: the immediate experience of the external world in the form of perceptions and the transformed thoughts. We surrender, as it were, completely to the present; our inner activity loses itself in the present. Then, however, this immediate activity continues. To begin with, it is not accessible to our consciousness. It sinks down into the subconscious but may be drawn to the surface again into memory. In what form, then, does it exist in us? This is a point that can be explained only by a direct view attainable in Imagination. A person who honestly pursues his way in his scientific striving cannot help but admit to himself that the moment the riddle of memory confronts him he cannot advance another step in his research. For due to the fact that the experiences of the immediate present sink down into the subconscious, they become inaccessible to ordinary consciousness; they cannot be traced further. But when we work in a corresponding way upon the human soul by means of the soul-spiritual exercises that have frequently been discussed in my lectures, we reach a stage where we no longer lose sight of the continuations of our direct life of perceptions and thoughts into conceptions that make memories possible. I have often explained to you that the first result of an ascent to Imaginative thinking is to have before your soul, as a mighty life-tableau, all your experiences since birth."

Bittersweet vine. I prefer the appearance of the Maple Tree over the vine, and I also know that the hedge-trimmers can take care of the problem, but it may be more efficient to cut back the Maple rather than try to cut down multiple examples of the fast-growing vines. But in this whole process of perception and knowledge we must come to terms with the whole life-apparatus which functions in each curling red leaf of the Japanese maple as it becomes known. We have -

1) the spirit of the maple itself,

2) the concept which in human thinking is inside the spirit of the maple leaf itself (as part of a rhythmic flow of going in and out, of world becoming man, and man becoming world),

3) the lit-up forms of human knowledge about and links between the idea of the Japanese maple and the Asiatic Bittersweet vine on the virtual encyclopedia planes. This is where the chain of inference flows.

4) the surging life passing from the spiritual archetype into the etheric world, streaming with living color and tone,

5) my external perception, solidifying colors and orientations, slicing up time and forgetting the spirit.

I can devote my heart as an organ of perception to the spiritual reality of this wholeness. In real spiritual scientific research, I look back then at all of my moral failings with complete and neutral accuracy, feeling the cosmic shame. I feel my empty loneliness, but also perceive the empty world warmth of space. And the human I as a spirit is coursing through the whole of nature, as well as the will and feeling of the human. Regarding the problem of the Maple and the Vine, I see that my everyday self is thinking through an inference chain by means of a deadening process of head-brain-representing in little images in the mind's small local subject-eye. It moves from place to place in the subjective mental plane by using the multiple tentacles of the fallen spirit of the head. In such moments, I realize that I have never considered the spiritual being of the Asiatic Bittersweet at all. I cut it down without ever even knowing what it is. I am empty and full.

Part of the river of inference is dammed up and part is still filling up a virtual lake, ready for future irrigations. Yes, parts of our problems are always unsolved, but this allows us to grow in morality in parallel to our giant intellectual jumps. Lotze is searching for the ground of the apparent coherence and connection of heterogeneous elements in the process of logical thinking. Certainly, one uniting element and ground is the flexible substance (seen outside the body) of the light matrix or virtual encyclopedia. But there are lakes that are further out, where the concepts live as cosmic mountains behind the stars. Here the ground is the self-created negotiation between Spirits, and the human Spirit can set up a residence there, with Christ's kind teaching. What a good thing that the work is never complete.

Francis Herbert Bradley's Notion of Inference

Let us take a moment to interact with other ideas about the movement of inference. In *Principles of Logic*, Bradley says: "Every inference is the ideal self-development of a given object taken as real."[105] There is a helpful kernel of active idealism that is functioning here, even though he does not use the terminology of the 'irreal' from Husserl. An object in thinking can unroll in the ideal plane based on its own innate character. Yet it is understood to be part of the real world and also connected to the whole world. Wolf and Blunt in their excellent article on 'Logic' from the 1911 *Encyclopedia Britannica* give their interpretation of Bradley: "The given object is an ideal content before us and it is taken to be real as being in one with reality, or the real universe. The possibility of inference rests upon the fact that the object is not only itself, but is also contained as an element in the whole; in fact, it is itself only as being so contained. From the nature of the case, inference must always be incomplete and subject to unknown conditions."[106]

Inference would be impossible without an intimate connectivity between ideas. But it would also be impossible if the truth available in each concept did not unfold its meaning out of its own essential sphere. If one concept disappeared entirely into another, there

---

[105] p 598
[106] p 329

could be no consistency or consequential development and progress of thinking. Such consistency does not exclude growth, change, inner differentiation and openness toward the unthought. There are a tremendously large number of inputs through which the flexible proto-substance of the etheric encyclopedia can be transformed, shaped, twisted, unraveled, disconnected, and reconnected, added to, and so on, without harming the universal process. In this way, this zone of human knowledge is a living supersensible field that is a creative artwork. One does not immediately see the effects of changes in this artwork in the sense world. Some effects never appear, and some will only appear in the future. Thank God that when I think of the concept of 'elephant' linked to the concept of 'lightning,' I do not immediately change the universe and bring an elephant made of lightning bolts into actual sensible existence. It is also amazing that thinking can move and transform at all. Who moves the event of thinking over the concept planes, in the midst of the continual freezing and thawing of morality and the firmly striding judgment furnaces? It is I. *In-fer-o.* My I is carried in by the vast thinking of the Spirit Word.

We find that in Bradley and his English interpreters, there is an element of logical inference which is unseen and must be viewed and walked in virtual intuition. All thinkers are in reality walking in logic strides with large steps and knitting with root-hands in multiple jet-streams in the etheric world. It is time for humanity to wake up to this real state of affairs. We can slowly learn how to consciously work, think, create and move in this world. Ben-Aharon describes many different aspects of this new etheric art in *Cognitive Yoga:*

> On the earth we are weighed down by physical gravity and tied to our bodies through their physical mass attracted by the whole physical body of the earth. In the etheric world, we are given one-sidedly to the infinite levitational attraction of the cosmic etheric forces of light...In properly undertaken spiritual scientific development, we want to be able to create and maintain, actively, a balanced and poised position in the etheric world, without being involuntarily dispersed and assimilated by the forces of this world. But in the etheric world the only force that can create gravity is the spiritual essence of what on earth is true morality. Moral gravity is absolutely needed as a basis for balanced down-rightness and walking-flying in the etheric fields.[107]

As we learn how to stand upright, speak, and walk in this growing etheric world with our new consciousness, we must learn that a new living logic can remain within humane bounds. Each person must deeply experience that the content of thinking must remain connected to the moral and ethical pulsing life of the soul and spiritual worlds. If not, every deductive, inductive, or abductive inference will be ultimately and essentially untrue, regardless of its truth table. In such cases we would become morally lame in the etheric world. Our personal memory,

---

[107] *Cognitive Yoga* pp 197-198

stored in swirls of life all throughout the human body, is not a complete copy of the thinking-world-planes, but rather a local and smaller constellation, which the personal subject finds useful. No doubt, our sense of self is a priceless possession. Unfortunately, in normal consciousness, the existence of the virtual blockchain or flexible inference field is not recognized or acknowledged, and the personal subject, operating with dead nodes, does not recognize the moral implications of only extracting one side of the story. Generally speaking, automata perform calculations in our personal life. Furthermore, the karmic walk of the spiritual process of drawing conclusions through the continual adjustment of moral balance is even less conscious. My wakening sense of the spiritual I AM of the other person creates a living major premise (sent out before – *pre-missus*) to ground all of the conclusions I draw in my sense of equilibrium, standing upright with him in his vertical spirit-light. The wholeness of a human spiritual logic provides etheric locomotion. The heart's blood that awakens in seeing the immoral consequences of our personal viewpoints is also frightfully absent in normal consciousness. Where is the blood of love and sacrifice on Deleuze's planes of immanence? Deleuze and Guattari's schizo-philosophical personas do not create the moral balance to walk with clear consciousness in the new life-world. Their work is very helpful in escaping from the Husserlian bubble, but it has its unbalanced tendencies. A spirit-self pouring out love must walk the living world-fire of true inference. Spiritual logic creates the opportunity for us to help carry the cross for one another. This is the higher critique of reason: that each move in thinking must face death resurrected by love.

Our subjective extraction from the proto-matrix also ignores another essential aspect: we are not the only ones plugged into the flexible light substance of human thinking. The angelic hierarchies are also interspersed and co-participants in the creation of cosmic knowledge. They are the grandparents of every concept. They live inside their offspring today. They are therefore co-painting and intensely creating in a much wider vista than humans are. They find themselves reversed, killed, and forgotten in the process of human 'thinking,' which unconsciously molds the virtual inference chain of proto-thinking light, but then extracts symbolic architecture, mere letters, or ghostly memories into a dead personal space, a dead electric-bio factory, centered in the human central nervous system. The luciferic spirits want to fly off with this light-filled hyper-field, where I can imagine anything I want, living in pure light in far off 'ancestral fields' (Goethe). The ahrimanic spirits want to pretend that the extract is the only real thing, and indeed can be produced by mineral and electro-magnetic operations. Can we find the middle?

We spiritually remember what is most alive in human knowledge by experiencing how we ourselves are connected with the whole process of universal life, wisdom, and love as well as with every element of natural law. We are woven into the elementals. This is dimly reflected in Bradley's notion that inference can only take place by the fact that one step or movement in thinking and one concept can be immediately connected to another. A tremendous and neutral flexibility exists in the fractal folds of the virtual knowledge-ocean, and openness as well as more space for connectivity must always be present in each part of the whole blockchain. Any idea can connect anywhere else, immediately. This is part of the immediate and universal copying or reproductive principle alive in the etheric (of course, the repetition comes to local terminations, like the echo that dies away, the growth of leaves which comes to the apex and waits for the flower, and the objects on the horizon which condense into a point).[108] But, as Bradley's interpreters point out, there is always an openness to a future which is not yet pre-printed in the virtual blockchain. In the realm of supersensible research and spiritual development, it is precisely this futural openness which can offer us a transition to the truly spiritual element in thinking, which takes place outside of our subjective control, in the spiritual life on the yonder side of the proto-light matrix. Ben-Aharon gives us an inspiring look into the deepest reality of human spiritual knowledge, which becomes

---

[108] Husserl glimpses a reflection of the reproductive and copying function of the etheric world in this moment, "As soon as an open horizon of like objects is present to consciousness as a horizon of presumptively actual and really possible objects, and as soon as it becomes intuitive as an open infinity, it gives itself as *an infinitude of particularizations of the SAME universal*...Thus it is evident that *the universal is not bound to any particular actuality.*" EJ, p 82

creative in the new Earthly-human sun growing this
very minute:

> This sphere of the spirit of knowledge and truth,
> aglow with the human-Christ created flames of
> spiritualized love in the depths, illuminated
> outwardly by the astral light pictures of world-
> thoughts, is opened in and through human eyes.
> Where objectified old cosmic space dies in our
> physical sense in-breathing as devitalized living
> time, and where sprouting sense-life produces in
> etheric sight majestic world-pictures through the
> formative forces of conscious human Imagination,
> man acquires the conscious capacity to imprint
> them – member them – into the planet's garments
> of resurrection.[109]

All of the work we are trying to achieve in the
spiritual life of this book is to contribute to the shaping
of the resurrection garments of a new humanity and
new earth. Can we weave a tapestry from the human
side while the spirits weave on the cosmic side? The
clothes that we have knit into the light-garment of
thought can be elevated as a blossoming gift, if They
accept it. Each axiom and deduction and personal
memory can provide rich compost in the new fields.
Husserl's thought has his part to play in this, and so
does every other thinker, whether he is Lotze, Wolf,
Foucault, or Bradley. The mother, Philosophia, has
many gifts to fertilize our humble etheric plantings
below and above. These plantings can blossom forth
from our quantitative and qualitative multiplicity in

---

[109] *The New Experience of the Supersensible*, pp 121-122

which we live our life. We can also look at this matter from the sub-earthly side, by Imaginatively viewing the whole man in his reasoning and counting activity. Steiner says,

> Out of our own inner being we bring everything which we introduce into the outer world as thoughts... In this connection we will consider the human being as a 'head-man,' we will consider him from the point of view of his head organization. He surveys the tapestry of the senses. Interwoven with this tapestry of the senses is all that we are able to acquire through the medium of thinking; and between this and what is contained in our own inner being there is a certain connection, a kind of sub-earthly connection. This is how it comes about that we draw forth from our inner being in the form of thought-life what we no longer perceive in the outer world owing to the fact that it has become part of us ourselves. This we incorporate into the outer world. Take counting for instance. There is no counting in the outer world. The laws underlying counting are contained in our own inner being. But that they are in accordance with truth depends upon the fact that between the potential qualities inherent in the outer world and our own earthly laws there is a sub-earthly connection going on below the surface, below the merely physical side of things. Hence, we derive the laws of number from our own inner being, and these laws are in harmony with what exists outside us. But the way does not lie through our eyes, through our senses, but through our whole organism. All that we develop by virtue of our humanity is developed out of the whole human

207

being. It is not true that we learn to comprehend Natural Law by means of the senses. We understand it with our whole human being.[110]

Thus, we weave on both sides, bringing the spiritual thinking down with us to the earth from before birth and then expanding our etheric body out to meet with the upright spiritual thinking in various levels of conscious participation. We can learn how to walk in self-conscious quantitative moral folds (let us recall that the '*plicare*' in multi-plication and im-plication means 'to fold'). We grow in pure acceleration and harmonic oscillation with the spiritual beings through comprehending, viewing and co-creating with the intermediate imaginative fields of human-spiritual world breathing: in-perceiving, out-knowing. In world-heart-harmony and wholeness, we bend to the new rice fields, strolling through the mud and water, planting new concepts with love.

Logical Laws and Spiritual Logical Laws: Implication and Disjunction on both sides

The whole point of this endeavor is to show that the forms of logical judgments in physical

---

[110] July 15, 1921 GA 205

consciousness do not by themselves exhaust the complete organic and living reality of thinking itself. If we are to carry and free our frozen laws of empirical and symbolic thinking (such as the rules of sentential logic) and clean them and plant them in spiritual experience, we have to experience some aspects more clearly, more warmly and more livingly. We must be conscious of every rice-sprout as we plant it in the watery mud. For an example, let us focus on the well-known possibility of replacing the essential logical form of 'material implication' $P \supset Q$, with $\sim P \vee Q$, which is possible in terms of the sheer formal rules of sentential logic. Their truth tables are identical. An example of the first hypothetical form would be that if Nellie's car is in the garage, she must be home (if P then Q). However, this major premise is the same as saying that there are two mutually exclusive possibilities: either the car is not in the garage or she is home (therefore $\sim P \vee Q$). This is true, given the narrow circumstances. Another example - if it is below 32 degrees then the water in the bowl outside is ice. This is the equivalent of 'either it is not below 32 or the water is frozen.' However, when it comes to truly thinking an organic living content, the reality must always overcome the form. Even if the form is logical, this does not mean that one is thinking livingly and organically, since errors in regard to understanding the full nature of reality can easily arise in the judgments themselves. This concerns the larger sense of Truth, beyond mere formal consistency, in terms of the interconnection of elements in a syllogism. "If the movie has 'Star Wars' in the title, it is a good film" is constructed according to proper logical form, but the truth of the matter can obviously be different.

Let us try to dig deeper into Truth in the larger sense. For example, it must be the case that spiritual laws are always the causes of what is perceived as material law. The work of the spiritual beings is the reality, and if this is not perceived or intuited, then all of the logical arguments that are associated with everyday thinking can be in grave error. For example, if I assume that a physical acorn can be created by other forces than those flowing in the etheric world and deriving from the nature beings and their work, then no matter what the form may be, my thinking will always be incorrect. In order for the material acorn to be perceived, the life forces must have created it first: $P \supset Q$ (or the equivalent $Q \lor {\sim}P$, either the etheric formative forces were active or there is no material acorn). If I create a plastic acorn and suggest that this is just as real and alive as the natural acorn, this is the equivalent in the laws of spiritual thinking of replacing $P \supset Q$ with $P \lor {\sim}Q$ (which is logically false). This is the equivalent in thinking organically and spiritually of trying to say that it is possible for Hopey and Maggie to be in Hoppers without being in California. (The corresponding spiritual argument based on real intuition is – the acorn is produced by spiritual life forces that are supersensible; there is a real or spiritual causal connection between this living whole and the perceptual aspect. It is also possible to say that the supersensible life might be active without the material form of the acorn yet existing. However, it is not possible to say that the material acorn can

210

exist without the underlying supersensible life forces. This is the spiritual equivalent of a logical fallacy). This is part of what is required to create a truly humane logic. We are not cutting off certain propositions from the standpoint of legalistic control, but rather we are carefully making sure that each thought is connected with real life, moral light, and creative warmth.

No doubt a thinker who limits her gaze to only material processes could protest − "Yes, but your original proposition about an 'etheric world' is wrong. I could still follow correct logical procedure by saying, the acorn is produced by genetic laws that can be measured and sensed. If these sense perceptible genetic influences did not exist, then the acorn would not grow. It is possible to still replace this cause and effect relationship with the disjunction $\sim P \lor Q$ and for our thinking to remain consistent; that is, either the genetic process underlying acorn growth is not active or there is an acorn." But, the point of our investigation is demonstrating how this materialist thought is false, even though it does not commit a logical fallacy. Its form is correct, but its content is false. Consistent and complete logical operations to not necessarily conform to reality.

Ahriman can always come up with another argument that denies the spirit, but this does not change the supersensible reality, in which the angels and the spiritual world are the real signified of all living thinking (even the thoughts which correctly apply to only physical processes!). We see this

211

incredibly successful attempt at crystallizing the merely formal in the Ahrimanic procession from Boolean algebra created in the 19th century to theoretical logic gates and then into vast systems of real electrical circuits. This is the spiritual attempt to rob the power of the free element in the human soul, from its legitimate supersensible, organic pulse, where it lives in an earthly spiritual cosmos, filled with soul. Material implication is caused by the virtual whole acting in every sensible part. When one begins to perceive supersensibly how the formative forces in the past have created the present sensible forms, then the representational logical law of material implication that functions in earthly logic transforms into a spiritual law of etheric implication. In this moment the etheric causes of natural events are revealed. One can follow this experience to comprehend that spiritual implication in general means that each judgment is super-naturally folded into the wholeness of the world of thought.

On the other hand, Disjunction is caused by the will operating in thinking. This disjunction becomes solidified in the representation of separated objects in normal consciousness. It then operates sub-consciously in every perception. So, I normally perceive that each car on the road is a different vehicle. The idea of the excluded middle (which spiritually speaking is built out of a web that is completely connected) is formed out of this Ahrimanic consciousness living in our heads. But as Deleuze has already taught us, a disjunctive synthesis (or a

mending of what is asunder) is functional in the
virtual or life plane.

Let us also focus on the center of all spiritualized
thinking, which is the Spiritual I of all humanity, who
gives the first creative impulse to earth and heaven to
both die and resurrect the true spiritual impulses alive
in the world, and in thinking. Christ is both the beacon
and the source of the I who thinks, and who thinks in
me. I receive the Spiritual Junction of true life and He
is implied and multiplied in me and my spiritual
community. His presence is the source of all true
intuition. It was His growing and intensifying
etherically active light, coming from the near future
that shone down into Fichte's never-ending
intellectual intuition. Fichte speaks truth when he
says, "Here everything depends on this: that each
person correctly identify with this insight, in this pure
light; if each one does, then nothing will happen to
extinguish this light again and to separate it from
yourself."[111]

---

[111] Some of the most important statements from Fichte's
lectures concern this living light intuited beyond the
concept in interior vision. Indeed you can even see this
active intuition in one of the drawings of Fichte's face:
"Regarding the entire distinction between the immanence
and e-manence of the production of an insight into light,
one must not forget that the same thing extends to the
insight and to the light itself. As before, the objective light
qua objective neither is, nor can become, the one true light.
Instead pure light enters insight under this aspect. But here
we have won this: *that the highest object is no longer
substance for itself, but light.* Substance is only the form of

213

light as self-sufficient. On the other hand, insight (subjectivity), actually the inner expression and life of light, disengages itself from the negation of the concept, and of division. Can you penetrate into the true midpoint more deeply in any other way? Into the entirely unique concept that is nevertheless required here?" p 53, J.G. Fichte, *Lectures on the Science of Knowing (1804).* Also this: "Here everything depends on this: that each person correctly identify with this insight, in this pure light; if each one does, then nothing will happen to extinguish this light again and to separate it from yourself. Each will see that the light exists only insofar as it intuits vitally in him, even intuits what has been established. The light exists only in living self-presentation as absolute insight, and whomever it does not thus grasp, hold, and fix in the place where we now stand, that one never arrives at the living light, no matter what apparent substitute for it he may have...Consideration of the light in its inner quality, and what follows from it, to which we will proceed after this step, is entirely different from this surrender and disappearance into the living light. This consideration as such will inwardly objectify and kill the light, as we will soon see more precisely. But first we said: only the light remains as eternal and absolute; and this [light], through its own inner immediate essence, sets down what is self-subsistent, and this latter loses its previously admitted immediacy to the light, whose product it is. But there is no life or expression of this light except through negating the concept, and hence through positing it. As we said, no expression or life of the light could arise unless we first unconditionally posit and see a life as a necessary determination of the light's being, without which no being is ever reached, except, that is, in the light itself—its essence in itself and its being, which can only be a living being. Thereby, however, what matters to us, since we add life to light, is that we have nevertheless divided the two, have therefore, as I said, actually killed the light's inner liveliness by our act of distinction; that is, by the concept." P. 60, wonderfully translated by Walter E. Wright, 2005

What is the relation between 1) consequence logic, 2) the truth of concepts and 3) the activity of understanding ideas without reference to external existence or validity?

As we are led by the moral light of the intuitively experienced I AM who creates thinking, let us now turn to consider from a logical point of view the following Husserlian question: 'What are the possible forms of all true judgments?'[112] This avenue of research concerns how we organize and link up individual concepts and judgments to make coherent and non-contradictory inferences. As we discussed earlier, Husserl calls this 'consequence-logic.' It is not yet concerned with whether the concepts and premises are true in themselves. He separates this operation from consequence logic and calls it 'truth-logic.' In our research in this section, we will also focus on the wider spiritual scientific context of consequence logic, and ask - How do we make coherent linkages in the planes of thought, considered from all angles – a) in normal consciousness, b) in viewing the subjective noematic and eidetic elements on the flowing light grid, c) in the impersonal Deleuzean planes at the threshold and d) across the threshold itself?

---

[112] He begins to research this question in FTL p 52

For example, imagine all possible coherent judgments that I could make concerning the concept of hydraulics and the pressure that is exerted through hoses to produce mechanical movement. Can I discover what controls the coherence of all possible judgments about the effectiveness of certain materials to create hydraulic hoses? Obviously, the coherence and non-contradictory forms of all judgments related to hydraulic hoses must in some sense conform to the basic physical laws that are operative in how liquid distributes pressure. Of course, I could know beforehand that there are logical fallacies which cannot produce valid arguments about any subject beforehand, for example, the fallacy of the undistributed middle or equivocation and so on. In general, when I try to force identity out of mere logical association, I end up with contradictory forms of judgments; for example, when I reason like this: All hydraulic hoses are tubes. All subways are tubes. Therefore, all hydraulic hoses are subways. But Husserl is also concerned with how the elements and meaning of hose and subway appear as evidence in the phenomenological reduction, progressing from vagueness to clarity and how my attention itself can move from focusing on many elements to just focusing on one (polythetic attention becoming monothetic).

Let us look more deeply into all sides of the processes in consciousness and thinking which allow the complete inner understanding or 'analysis' of concepts and their rational linking with one another. How do we mend what is asunder on the idea-planes

216

that are born from the formless spirit? What allows reasonable ordering of the self-differentiating blossom of archetypal concepts in the first place and can we view them and walk them with full saturation in the moral mode? How do I meet the spiritual beings who produce the distribution of pressure in fluid in our physical experience? Deleuze, Husserl and Steiner do not stop at the border of the merely formal logical combinatorial exercise which takes place in all of the logical systems arising after Boole and Frege. Yes, we can organize the abstract forms of judgments and basic moves of inference in symbolic logic and in circuits that function in a lock-tight manner, but this does not tell us about the origin and living element of human thinking as it is created and experienced. We can calculate pressure per square inch in a hydraulic system, but this does not tell us how the concepts in Pascal's law and its ramifications exist on the thought plane itself.

In *Formal and Transcendental Logic*, Husserl turns toward a phenomenological description of the idiosyncratic character of the intentional features which operate when a person is engaging in 'consequence logic.' Can we view the deep power that we possess to create and organize specific judgments out of prototypical essences of possible judgments that are seen eidetically from the inside? Husserl says:

> When can judgment-forms be grasped in original insight as eidetic universalities pertaining to judgments that can be made actually and properly? When do they, as such universalities, have ideal

217

"existence"?...The forms, as eidetic universalities, are eidetic laws. Pure analytics, we can say according to all this, is a science that seeks out systematically the primitive forms of judgments that can be judged in a complete activity proper, the "primitive operations" whereby such judgments can be varied syntactically, and the original modes of their connective (copulative, conjunctive) combination. Starting from these forms, operations, and modes of combination, and guided by the purely grammatical reiterations in the constructing of forms, pure analytics must trace, level by level, the resultant possibilities of constructing forms of judgments "proper", and in this fashion it must bring under laws the whole system of judgment-possibility within the sphere of distinctness — ideally speaking, by systematic construction of the existent forms.[113]

How does the original concept-mother produce her children, and what is the glue that holds her offspring together? What are all of the truth-rivers that can actually flow out of the original spring of rigorous human thought? He suggests that one of the powers or intuitive functions which operates during the mind's use of consequence logic, is the ability to understand the meaning of language and the propositions and concepts that function at a deeper level beyond mere phoneme or grapheme. In other words, Husserl continues to follow the guidance of grammatical and linguistic structures. When I listen to the ideas of another person who is discussing

---

[113] FTL pp 334 and 336

218

hydraulic hoses, I follow his thinking patterns, but I verify the correctness of his thinking patterns through the way he expresses them in language.

If we extend Husserl's ponderings, we find that the thinking-spirit has the faculties to 1) allow the meaning of a proposition to become fulfilled in categorial intuition by focusing on the conceptual content and the linking apparatus of reason itself and 2) the possibility of incorporating the individual concepts into the overall structure of ideas (by focusing on the process of logical incorporation as a self-conscious activity). Put more simply, we have the capacity to focus on the meaning and the linkages as a substance and we have the capacity to perform the linking itself. We have a reflective and an operational power. This second operational power that we naturally possess as thinkers is what Husserl calls 'a priori synthesis.' I can suggest new materials for hydraulic hoses that run a post-pounding machine, based on linking together a wide-variety of associative steps using my will-in-thinking on the virtual inference plane. If we follow a series of coherent judgments that we have made 1) to the threshold and then 2) across the threshold, we might ask how the fruit of our new creations in thinking can be linked up with the whole supersensible blockchain and then planted in the warm water of the new moral rice fields in the etheric world proper. How can the residue of the inference chains that have been coherently synthesized by the will-forces be spiritualized? Beyond the effectiveness of a new titanium and chromium hydraulic hose in real applications in the physical world of building fences, I am concerned here with how this dead subjective structure of representational thinking can be resurrected and elevated in spiritual consciousness across the threshold. This activity produces a wholeness in human life. Yes, I can create new types of hoses, build fences, and I can also create new spiritual life by working with the spiritual beings in the extended ecology of the supersensible earth.

Husserl is oriented toward the following question: How do I evaluate the coherency of a form of judgment - both beforehand and during the operations - based on direct witnessing and living inside of the pulse of the thinking fabric itself (and based on the fullest potential of the concepts involved), rather than based on external coherence of form? Is it impossible to link certain concepts together at all? Will some forms of grammatical expression and connection lead to incoherent or contradictory results? Many logicians have pondered the paradox of the round-square, but what about 'whom-moss?' Is a relative pronoun + noun structure possible when viewed eidetically in consequence logic? Are the limits of the English language different from the eidetic flow of 'whom-moss' and is it possible to experience 'whom-moss' in Deleuze's planes of immanence? Whom-moss seems impossibly fragmentary, where the antecedent of 'whom' is forgotten and therefore it remains impossible to tell exactly what 'moss' is being connected to. Is it possible to spiritualize this concept itself? How can I be confident that I have penetrated to all of the ramifications that are present in the interior of the concept (this is, its *spiritual-analytic* aspect)?

In transcendental phenomenology, this cannot be an abstract discussion or a mere mechanical operation of organizing truth tables, of drawing Venn diagrams, or creating circuits that are actualizations of logic gates. This can be investigated phenomenologically by beholding the eidetic pathways which are used by deductive reasoning through the supersensible thinking activity of humanity as a whole. To view it and live in it conceptually, one can say that there are giant inference rivers in the thought world, that operate according to 1) recognition of form, 2) belonging to a set, 3) combination, and 4) condensation of the previous steps. In regard to maintaining an element of rigor and balance in the multiple links, we have to also investigate the problems of biased habits, unknown unknowns, personal sympathies, incorrect range or scope, improper comparisons and so on. This shows the limit of the content of what can be included in the judgment form but not the form itself. I have to exclude issues which have nothing to do with the effectiveness of hydraulic hose materials, such as the insects in the area, or the color of the sky on a particular day. But if I never meet the spirits of the steel that are present in the current hoses, I am also only experiencing part of the issue.

If we move beyond the Husserlian eidetic realm, we can also behold the flowing and metamorphosis of the forms of meaning and their more lively and gentle archetypes lying behind the main inference rivers. Sometimes the living concepts, which exist like terrains and mountains behind or on the horizon in the distance behind the inference rivers, deposit their dead leaves or used up soil into the inference rivers and these deposits flow downstream logically, and then can be understood as miniature frozen forms in the heads of humans. Here all of the concepts become expanding roots, differentiating in new pulsing avenues, but we remain sober and awake in these zones of near extinguishment of memory and self-consciousness. It is important at this stage (since we need to learn how to transform the forces of death in thinking into new life in order to spiritualize anything) to look back at the head-centered process from the spiritual scientific side with more intimacy and understanding.

This interiorizing and representing in thinking (inside the small human physical sphere) is registered and viewed inside the head in a secure and consistent way by the coming together of the two etheric streams, one flowing down from the living concepts, one rising up from the heart and the places where memories are stored behind the heart and below the head. As Steiner indicates in *Esoteric Physiology*, it is only when these streams are held apart that one can begin to think outside the brain and body and begin the first steps of etheric cognition. Steiner says: "Thus we have in the brain, whenever a memory-picture or a representation of a thought wishes to form itself, two ether-currents, one coming from below and one from above, which oppose each other under the greatest possible tension, just as two electric currents oppose each other. If a balance is brought about between these two currents, then a concept has become a memory-picture or a thought-through mental image [*Gedächtnisvorstellung*] and has incorporated itself in the ether-body."[114]

When you hold the two currents apart for a time, then you can watch without falling asleep how, in the next moment, when you allow the two streams to touch again, you simultaneously form a mental picture with a feeling of security that also draws your mental vision back into the center of the brain. In this moment, the trap snaps closed and you believe that you are the inner self using thinking for your own subjective self-conscious processes. When the condensing and contracting forces coming down from the pineal area inscribe their chalk forms into the warm dimness of the pituitary activity below and a bit forward (almost like putting a needle on a record) the feeling of being inside a body is complete, and the ahrimanic-luciferic partnership has done its work. This is like the cherry on top of a vanilla-chocolate twist ice-cream cone. And boy, do we love eating the ice cream from the inside – yum yum! The spiritual reality is that we see very little of the whole process and misunderstood the moral and spiritual life behind real thinking altogether. You believe that you are thinking, but the connection of the two streams does nothing but consolidate the dead webs of the Ahrimanic double who lives alongside you, indeed as

---

[114] GA 128, lecture 4

you. Everyday consciousness is built on the fact that you can't see the way spiritual thinking beyond the confines of your skin is turned into a little fairy theater in your head by the joining of these two groups of streams. In fact, we only become conscious by this process of contracting, paralyzing, condensing, freezing, and linearization which kills spiritual reality. Until you really experience and see this no real anthroposophical research can begin, no matter how much you have meditated, etc. This is precisely what Steiner points out when he says, "But one should not confuse 'having thought images' with the working through of thought by means of thinking. Thought-images can arise in the soul in the same way as dreams or vague intimations. This is not thinking."[115] If you hold the two streams apart, you can find the middle space, where the pure duration of the real unknown thinking, feeling, and willing acts in you.

When you follow this process into the spiritual world, focusing on the concept of hydraulics, you find that the concept of pressure and fluid changes altogether. The way that the fluid can distribute its pressure throughout its whole substance in order to resist and push against the solid material forms, becomes a totally different reality there. There is now interpenetration of beings. There is always a virtual release valve, and the solidity of the edge of the hose that is necessary for all hydraulic functions in the physical world disappears. The ahrimanic solidity disappears in the etheric world. But this only concerns

---

[115] *Philosophy of Freedom*, revised addendum to chapter 3

the concept beings themselves. When we look at the question of consequence logic from this vantage point, we see that there can be self-created lines and clouds of fiery will that move through vast segments of the concept planes 'from underneath' or 'in between.' These quick elements of fiery will can ramify through all the terrains of concepts to hold together a coherent and rigorous organization of unfolding knowledge, that is all oriented toward what is possible coming from previous understandings and the inner potency of the prime concept, in this case, hydraulics. The will moves as anticipatory projection based on the innate possibilities of the concept being. Such a logical form then must also conform to the organic structure of the human organs. The dream logic where things change instantly into one another is not sufficient to produce an earthly human knowledge. It must be fully incorporated into the flow of time, life, and the incarnated experience of the organs, veins, blood, joints, nervous systems, skeleton and other features of the human individual body as a whole. With this insight, it becomes clear that medicine and logic can be joined in this one area. Spiritualized thinking is healing and nourishment. But remember that, from the viewpoint of the spiritual world, the small human body is woven throughout the whole solar system, and multiple spirits weave inside it. So, bodily organic logic is also planetary law. This is a deeper study that we cannot enter into in this book, but one does not even have to be clairvoyant to penetrate to the essence of the connection between the organs in the body and true world-thinking. However, this requires a step which can be difficult to understand: we can open our comprehension to the supersensible life that is connected with every written word in Steiner. The opening to a new form of spiritual scientific comprehension is enough to meet the wholeness of the spiritual beings and their activities. But this must be carefully distinguished from shuffling through dead representations. That is the biggest jump.[116]

---

[116] "People cannot arrive at the relation of the heart to the liver if they do not first acquire the method for it by means of a training in Spiritual Science. In earlier times people could say: the heart is related to the liver somewhat as the Sun to Mercury in the outer world; and man knew something of how this relationship of Sun to Mercury was drawn from the super-sensible world into the sense world. This is now no longer understood, nor can it ever be thoroughly understood if the foundation, the basic impulse for this comprehension, be not acquired from within. It is not through clairvoyance alone that man can make it his own. By clairvoyance the facts of Spiritual Science are investigated; but man acquires this sense when he enters with his whole thought and feeling into what has already been discovered by clairvoyant methods, and regulates his life accordingly. That is the essential point. What is of moment is *to study the conclusions of Spiritual Science*, not to satisfy a curiosity for clairvoyance. That must be emphasised again and again. For in the whole development of human culture, this application of the methods of Spiritual Science to outer life and to the knowledge of the great world, the world outside man, is of quite special importance. When we consider what we thus have to look upon as the original head-organisation, when we consider it in the course of our life, we see how it gradually becomes permeated with all in our organisation that is adapted to the world outside. Thus we must learn to understand the world outside man from man's own organism, from the human limb-organisation; and there, only such things as I have already hinted at can help us. I have shown the contrast that exists between the waking and sleeping conditions of man. These are contrasting conditions, and when one condition is passing over into the other,

Spiritualizing the Concept of Currency

Husserl did not recognize the deeper reality of the cosmic organology of logic. But we can look at precisely what he did accomplish. For him, the transition from logical thinking to phenomenological insight takes place when the meaning elements come to awareness in a fully saturated intuition or viewing of the sense of concepts in the thinking-terrain. This particulate substance on which the mental images and logical eidetic structures are projected seems to extend to infinity if it is not bypassed through moral development and heart thinking. When it is bypassed through the power of love dissolving its frozen power, we enter into another world, as our soul expands. In this moment we look back to find that the etheric grid is located fairly close to the physical body (in a spatial sense). In this moment we also recognize that every thought picture is a projection onto the dying light grid around the physical body, but that truly soul experiences and spiritual Imagination, Inspiration, and Intuition take place beyond this fabric of receptivity of light-forms used in personal thinking. It is important to also note that for Husserl part of the powers of human judgment concern the capacity to repeat the viewing of the identical essential concept or

---

that is to say, when we wake up and when we go to sleep, then we pass through a zero-point of our existence." (GA 201, lecture 10)

judgment again and again. For logical truth to consist, it is necessary for Husserl that the essential elements remain identical. But this quest for secure identity is problematic as has been shown by Derrida and Deleuze, among others. Can logic function, if the content of P is different every time I think it, even in a single syllogism? Is my father the same, every time I think of him? Is what was true of my sister yesterday, still true of her?

If we now carry this problem to the spiritual threshold and try to cross into direct spiritual experience and a co-working with our spiritual brothers and sisters as we think through this problem, we find the following. Let us start with an example. I am wondering whether I will receive a significant return on my investment on a particular cryptocurrency. Focusing on the synthetic activity of consequence logic, I create the following syllogism: if the developers and the team working on the development and implementation of the blockchain and the related apps are legitimate, and the app is used by the wider public and if I can buy when the price for the coin is rather low, I will receive a sufficient return on my investment in the future. In real instances, then, I investigate coin Y or project X and find that they seem to fulfill all of these requirements, therefore I make the judgment that I will receive a sufficient return on my investment in coin X or Y. We find that the general form of the argument is as simple as possible: If A then B; A, therefore B. But, of course the reality is much more complex.

There might be many reasons, of course, which could result in a financial loss of a part of my investment even if the form of my argument is valid and even if I am correct that all of the elements in my major premise are correct. For example, it might well be the case that the blockchain team is great and that millions use the app or the particular cryptocurrency, but nevertheless the investment, which only focuses on the buying and selling of the coin itself is not profitable. A company might turn a profit and be a good business and yet the stock still might not produce a high return on investment. These things are all possible along with many unforeseen consequences that inductive generalizations cannot predict. Financial markets often follow irrational psychological trends, as is well known.

But now let us focus and go inward one step. What is the value of the phenomenological turn? What is the value of intuiting the meaning of the concepts with a direct and full saturation in the Husserlian sense? First, it is important to distinguish between pure perception and thinking. I learn nothing from the white papers of businesses from merely staring at the computer screen and seeing black lines on white paper. I can only synthesize the various lines into something meaningful in the first place through thinking. Seeing random faces of the 'development team' means nothing until thinking combines the ideas of their accomplishments together into the concept of a company or a business, and their successful cooperation. A green piece of paper means nothing if I do not consciously understand the meaning of the concept of currency. As Heraclitus rightly pointed out, a donkey will choose hay over gold. The donkey obviously perceives the gold, but does not think the significance of the value of gold in the economic processes of humans.

Now, if I look into the meaning structures and experiences themselves, if I look into the direct evidence of flowing in the experience of thinking the concept of currency, this is different from making a decision about the value of a particular investment. The externally perceptible elements are gone, and in the Husserlian sense, I can intuit the concept of currency. When I look into the noematic appearance of the concept of currency, I find that if I can set aside the specific memory images or received ideas about currency, I can find an element that is activated in pure thinking. I can note that there is a material and a quality associated with the viewing of the concept of currency. I can differentiate the meaning of currency as a medium or a representation of value that can be exchanged in a local economy from the concept of a nut, for example. I find that there is a noetic act or a thinking act which can move from observing the concept of a nut and can go back to the meaning-limits of a currency. I want to keep the two circles of the Venn diagram from overlapping, but I am a witness to the causal meaning scope of each concept in full saturation. For example, I can trace and locate the precise boundary in the viewing of concepts between green paper and real US dollars. We might be fooled by a counterfeit dollar in our perception, but we can always differentiate between the concept of a real dollar and the concept of a counterfeit dollar. There is a meaning-boundary between the two. What power in me is able to think the difference between the two? How do I return to the same concept? Who thinks and how does the thinker weave through time and memories while retaining an identity? These are Husserlian questions.

Steiner would go further and suggest that when the thinker or the I AM wakes up and observes the very activity of creating, combining, differentiating, and linking up concepts in the non-imagistic, non-subjective thinking sphere, another realm opens up that is beyond the physical (and the dying etheric grid of representations) altogether. This can happen if we are able to both hold the two currents in the head apart, and also activate the middle zone with devotion, morality, spiritual scientific fundamental exercises, and self-knowledge. We can experience the spiritual I or thinker outside the body, thinking in the midst of a world of flowing concepts, moods, and Imaginative folds and world-large Imaginative pictures that are supersensible. The whole 'body' is involved in this process not just the head. Thinking is then recognized as an activity that precedes all experience of concepts, and creates concepts by which it orders reality in terms of inner, outer, space, time, quantity, body, etc. The observation of self-thinking activity surfs on top of the observation of the concepts created through thinking, and the emotion and will clouds. We can also become aware of the warm, will-walker, and the spirit-heart gestures, which constitute the soul and spiritual logical actor. The complete logic farmer is

231

present, able to morally walk and plant in his fields, with the sun shining down, supersensibly.

But the investor might argue that neither the Husserlian nor the further Anthroposophical dimension improve her capacity to make a winning trade. She might look on the phenomenological move as perhaps opening up a new realm of experience but as a useless addition which adds nothing to her clarity of judgment, like someone who creates a glass dishwasher that is visible on all sides to watch the moment by moment workings of the spraying water, dispensing of soap and rotating arms. Does this really help the dishes get any cleaner? A person thinking in the same vein would argue that I can drive a car without knowing how internal combustion works or how rubber is made. Phenomenological viewing and the further spiritualization of thinking do not provide any 'real world' advantage, they might say. One type of investor might go so far as to suggest that if you really believed in spirits, you should command them to show you the future prices of the cryptocurrency or stock markets.

On the other side, the visionary would try to tell the investor that the amazing landscapes and the blissful feelings that one experiences as you learn to see intense and vast images in the mind's eye are far more valuable than making money in the external world. Once a person has seen the incredible architecture and the impossibly beautiful lands that are within our inward vision, they can never turn back to the 'dark and dirty earth, with its greedy people.'

This might lead to a new age conversion, where one could become a dharma bum. Husserl does not go this far, but his phenomenology could be distorted into connections with the mystic visionary. Steiner goes in an entirely different direction, but his ideas can also be distorted into a support for personal, subjective soul development.

But if we can truly penetrate into the middle zone between these two extremes, we can find that the spiritualized thinking, which experiences the freedom of the I who thinks both inside the body and outside the body without leaving the earth behind, can experience the most valuable element in the truly moral dimension. Through the spiritualization of thinking, which passes beyond the eidos in Husserl's works, we come to see out the back of the flexible and open concepts of currency. We find an element in the concept of currency that we never noted before, because we never recognized how our own subjective greed, love of personal comfort, and our hatred of other people were wrapped in the experience of investment in the first place. We can now look back at our whole constitution of soul, feelings, desires, and body as a stranger and can see how that aspect of inwardness distorted all of the meanings of all of the concepts.[117] The reversal was inside every meaning.

---

[117] Scheler shows his real contribution to the evolution of phenomenology in his recognition of this reality, "What is called [by Nietzsche] 'falsification of the value tablets', 're-interpretation,' or 'transvaluation' should not be mistaken for conscious lying. Indeed, it goes beyond the sphere of judging. It is not that the positive value is felt as such and

Now the spiritual event of the I waking up and being woken up inside the spiritual world of thinking as living beings co-working, wrestling, and producing world consecration, is recognized for the first time. We note that currency is primarily a spiritual living idea of humans giving and taking in a community of soul and spiritual exchange. I become something else by receiving your karmic treasure. This is a different idea than accumulating material wealth or buying material objects to support my ego being. All the potential of trying to pass on spiritual treasure and the most intimate gift to one another rises across the threshold. We hold a gift in our spirit-self which allows the other to find his or her way into a higher grasp of his own self. The spiritual currency is the

---

that it is merely declared to be 'bad.' Beyond all conscious lying and falsifying, there is a deeper 'organic mendacity.' Here the falsification is not formed in consciousness, but at the same stage of the mental process as the impressions and value feelings themselves: *on the road* of experience into consciousness. There is 'organic mendacity' whenever a man's mind admits only those impressions which serve his 'interest' or his instinctive attitude. Already in the process of mental reproduction and recollection, the contents of his experience are modified in this direction. He who is 'mendacious' has no need to lie! In his case, the automatic process of forming recollections, impressions, and feelings is involuntarily slanted, so that conscious falsification becomes unnecessary. Indeed, the most honest and upright convictions may prevail in the periphery of consciousness. The apprehension of values follows this pattern, to the point of their complete reversal. The value judgment is based on this original 'falsification.'" *Ressentiment*, p 78. Scheler has solved the riddle of the Cretan who says 'Everything that I am telling you is a lie."

exchange of transformed consciousness arising through meeting the other. I may even take on the debt of the other as we enter into a spiritual community in spiritual and soul wakefulness. This insight into the spiritual concept of money can then totally change our relationship to investment and the notion of earthly money. Can I invest my own spiritual quest in your spiritual awakening and growth? None of these moral elements are really recognized by Husserl. Yes, he is not concerned with getting rich, but on the other hand, he does not recognize the cosmic supersensible and moral struggle through which Michael and his co-workers are trying to lift up and transform the merely *earthly picture-reasoning through memory images inside and around a body* into something else: a co-working with the true spirit of humanity and the angelic hierarchies, to transform the evil in ourselves and the world. We need to get real with one another. The deeper meanings and a truer insight into the whole of life is only found through spiritual scientific consciousness. This has nothing to do with following a particular guru or losing my own independence. The spiritual scientist can understand and utilize the ideas of the earthly investor or mechanic as well as the phenomenological researcher, but not vice versa. Multiple new currencies can arise, with the highest beauty of art and utility. I give part of myself to the other, when I give her supersensible 'currency,' and she gives part of herself to me. We need the gift of the Other to find the deepest answer to 'making a living.'

Chapter 10 - The Riddle of the Transcendental I and its Possible Immortality in Husserl

There were moments in Husserl's life and writings where he reached a deep sense of clarity regarding the nature of the Self. It was rare that Husserl gave public voice to his personal beliefs about the possibility of an existence before birth or after death, but he did have conversations with his friends and students about these topics. Cairns reports the following conversation from the 1930s with Husserl and another student, Eugen Fink:

> The transcendental ego which stands in *Gemeinschaft* [companionship] with itself, which constitutes and has a world, is a wakeful ego. Its continuity points back to a *Stiftung* [institution or endowment] through wakeful life, either its own life or that of some other self. The world is established through a wakeful transcendental subjectivity. Now, waking life is perhaps broken by pauses of sleep, when the ego is no longer active (dreaming is itself a break in sleep, a sort of wakefulness, when 'sleep' is taken in this sense). But the continuity is still 'there' in the sense that it can be awakened. Death, however, makes awakening impossible, but the question arises, does death destroy the continuity?...We are faced with the fact that a newborn child (a newly 'waking' transcendental ego)

may have determinations of character, i.e., determinations [that seem to be] handed down, which can be awakened in him, though he may never have acquired them himself nor gained them through communication with other subjects with whom he has a common world intercourse...Husserl pointed out that these considerations were in themselves merely indications for a direction in which one may work further, through concrete analyses revealing essential potentialities and perhaps essential necessities.[118]

Husserl's phenomenology was faced with the problem of sleep and death as interruptions in the enduring construction of meaning and understanding performed by the human being in relationship to her life and world. Every morning, I awake as the same person and with memories of the past. This provides difficulty for any Cartesian philosophical approach. In this conversation, he ponders dreaming consciousness, which could hold the key to a hidden unbroken continuity. He points out that if no continuity existed, it would be logically impossible for us to wake up again as the same human. Our human civilization depends on such continuity. He also mentions a fact that everyone recognizes: children are born with talents and characters which could never be explained by materialistic genetics. But we generally awake to self-consciousness in childhood with no memory of any previous life. In this case, as spiritual science teaches us, the continuity is only perceivable

---

[118] Cairns, Dorion, *Conversations with Husserl and Fink.* The Hague: Martinus Nijhoff, 1976, pp 68-69, translation modified

at a much deeper level. The most reasonable explanation for child prodigies, as Steiner pointed out, is in the idea of reincarnation, in which the spiritual self in its highest aspect (*der Geistesmensch*) gives birth to a new earthly human incarnation, in accordance with spiritual law.[119] Husserl showed no interest in reincarnation. His search for continuity could only penetrate as far as the intentional realm of pure meaning, but in the endurance of the consciousness of the flow of time, he thought that he had found something capable of lasting beyond the death of our personality and bodies. Did he? Let us follow his beautiful struggle:

> Even if the presently enduring unitary object or event can cease, the process of the enduring itself cannot come to a halt. The enduring is immortal. When the tone ceases, precisely something else is there in its stead as the enduring present. It could be the case that the world does not exist...in contrast, it is absurd that immanent being (the present being that is being constituted in the enduring) would cease: it is inconceivable that everything would come to a halt and that then there would be nothing...The cessation itself as the cessation of the object, presupposes a non-cessation, namely, consciousness to which the cessation is given.[120]...This implies that the process of

---

[119] Of course, Steiner did not only logically deduce this hidden continuity, but followed through the spiritual destinies of a large number of individualities, through spiritual scientific research. See Steiner's 8 volume work on *Karmic Relationships* (GA 240)

[120] Connect this with the Goethean element in the 3rd degree of the Misraim Service in Steiner's GA 265 –

living on, and the ego that lives on, are immortal – *nota bene*, the pure transcendental ego, and not the empirical ego in the world that can very well die. We do not at all deny the latter's death, its corporeal decomposition...[But] every Now leaves a trail of retentions; we cannot conceive of a Now that does not already have retentions...The nothing prior to the beginning already presupposes a something with which it could conflict. There can be an emptiness prior to the beginning, an undifferentiated, monotone, mute stupefaction, but even this is something past, and has the essential structure of something temporal...Upon closer inspection, we see that remembering is a modification of perception as an act, that is, it presupposes a wakeful I...Every past is an enduring past that varies with the present to which it belongs. But with the change of these modes, there is the one unending time to the extent that it is already past, and every position, every expanse of this time, is absolutely fixed and identical, namely, identifiable again and again with complete certainty as the same. Consequently, transcendental life and the transcendental ego cannot be born; only the human being in the world can be born. The ego as transcendental ego was eternal; I am now, and belonging to this Now is a horizon of the past that can be unraveled into infinity. And this means precisely, the ego was eternal...What is futural will be past after it was present...This structure of the future thus fashions the futural bent of subjectively oriented time, oriented toward the mobile zero-point of the temporal orientation, toward the Now, in relation to which I

"Think about the end; think about death; everything physical is transitory." This moment of paradox is a wonderful little key to open the spirit.

stand as a perceiving ego, as the ego of the present....in a certain respect every human-ego harbors its transcendental ego, and this does not die and does not arise; it is an eternal being in the process of becoming.[121]

We find here a wonderful opportunity to explore the possibility of really building a bridge to the spiritual world by means of the new entry point of Anthroposophy. Through stripping away aspect after aspect in his phenomenological reduction, Husserl has located an intuition of the continuous flow of the fullness of living time, before it becomes broken into particular moments and fragmented representations and objects attached to my own personal life. It would be fruitful to compare this passage to the incredible analyses of memory in Bergson's *Matter and Memory* and *Time and Free Will.* I am sure that Bergson and Husserl would have many disagreements (Heidegger dismisses Bergson much too superficially in *Being and Time*), but there is no doubt that they have both uncovered the experience of pure duration. Pure duration is not something that can really be represented in everyday consciousness; it requires a deeper level of awareness that melts or sets aside the normal ways of thinking about time. It requires that warm Goethean flow of merging together with nature. It requires that Deleuzean coolness of digging one's mental roots in the dirt. Ben-Aharon has taught us

---

[121] It is really necessary to read this remarkable analysis as a whole. It is found in APAS pp 466-471 from 1922-23.

240

how to achieve it by separating percepts and concepts.[122]

One can hardly overestimate the damage that is caused by the condensation of the concept of time into a representation of a 'time-line' that is sketched on the board to explain time to children in elementary school. I am shocked when I realize just how much that one seemingly small representation has infiltrated all of my adult notions about the reality of time. Of course, being able to calculate precise quantitative relationships is important, but this representation of linear time is false on all fronts, whether empirical or spiritual scientific. Quantitative division is in reality created by the dying crystallization streams of consciousness itself, which takes the archetypal spiritual harmony and universal connectivity and breaks it into infinite little pieces, slicing apart life and light. The movement and rhythm of the cosmic spiritual life is projected onto a dead clock, or onto a cell-phone screen. But Goethe gives us renewed hope of putting humpty-dumpty back together again, "What higher synthesis is there than a living organism? Why would we submit ourselves to the torments of anatomy, physiology, and psychology if not to reach some concept of the whole, a concept which can always restore itself to wholeness no matter how it is torn to pieces."[123]

---

[122] See *Cognitive Yoga* p 26
[123] "Analysis and Synthesis," translated by Douglas Miller

Let us return to Husserl's quote above. First of all, we might ask the question – is Husserl correct in what he says? The living answer depends on whether we can really struggle with the threshold between our own personal life experience and the real spiritual world which lies on the other side of the threshold. Even though Husserl dives down into an underlying experience of time, and makes correct logical deductions, he also fails to walk through the door of the nothing that he meets in the past and the zero-point that he meets in the now and in the future.[124] He fails to experience the real shocking difference between all of my hopes for immortality and the real spiritual experience of living beyond death and being resurrected beyond my subjective wishes, by the spiritual world. The opening of the doors to the experience of the spiritual world, certainly lives in the highest sense with the awakening of the I AM, but there is a vast chasm between the endless duration that he projects into infinity, and the real death experience that one must have to truly experience the spiritual world as a reality. He glimpses something higher than his 'empirical ego,' but his so-called 'transcendental ego' does not penetrate even to the level of moral intuition as performed in Steiner's epistemological works. Husserl never leaves his subjective bubble, unfortunately. This is always the

---

[124] Steiner says, "In reality, the Nothingness is, as in the words of Faust, the "All," but it presents itself as a Nothingness. It is a question of crossing an abyss...In this epoch, as regards the Christ Event, as regards the deeper, more intimate religious questions, men are clearly facing a Nothingness." (GA 217)

problem with Husserl and indeed neither Bergson nor Heidegger ever progressed beyond this (subjectively) true and valid experience of the pure flow of time and memory, which lies at the boundary of personal consciousness. All of them were becoming aware to one degree or another of their etheric bodies as a flowing stream of time and memory, but they could not cross the threshold into the world-ether proper, the soul outside themselves, nor the spiritual I. The living thinking and the experience of the I standing in thinking that is described in Steiner's *Philosophy of Freedom* is absolutely NOT the pure transcendental ego that Husserl describes and experiences here. I have experienced both and have carefully compared them over many years. The difference is the radical one between living inside the body and stepping outside it. Until you have experienced it, you can hardly imagine the difference. The problem is caused by both a failure of consciousness and a failure of morality on the part of all attempts at phenomenological reflection.

It is the same problem that was described in many different ways in my book, *The Resurrection of Thinking*. I understand Husserl's problem quite well, because I also followed his path for many years, even as I began to study anthroposophy. It is quite possible to study Steiner for a whole lifetime, and to begin 'meditation' without really penetrating beyond the threshold. But without crossing the threshold through spiritualizing thinking with devotion, one can only receive 'clairvoyant faculties' from lucifer or ahrimanic spirits. Such an approach, which remains

243

bound in the illusion of subjectivity, has nothing to do with real Anthroposophy. Lucifer and Ahriman can use everything, even Steiner's dead words in your brain, to their advantage. There is a vast difference between the world revealed through Lucifer's work in the soul and the real spiritual world revealed through the true Christ spirit, the contemporary work of Michael, and the living spirit and soul of Anthroposophia. Husserl's mathematical training prevented him from straying too far into fantasy, but on the other hand, he could not really penetrate or be broken through by the true Christ spirit as the fully modern entranceway to the spiritual world appropriate to a healthy humanity. Such a step requires developing the heart as a cognitive organ.

As Levinas discovered, there is a real moral rupture that is experienced when I truly bump into the other. There is a repressed immorality at the bottom of all of my projects to maintain my subjectivity in the face of the true other who threatens to break through all of my security. The Other (the spirit of the other human, or the spiritual world as a whole) is there before my subjective self. The spirit of the other human being, as I awake to my inner ethical relationship to him or her, awakens a thought of the infinite beyond normal consciousness. [125] It is certainly

---

[125] The whole of Levinas's demonstration of the limits of Husserl are evident in this one passage from 1984: "The idea of the infinite – an exceptional and unique idea which, according to Descartes, is the thought addressed to God. It is a thought which, in its phenomenology, does not allow itself to be reduced, without remainder, to the act of

possible to awaken a free thinker who operates before subject and object in the sense of Steiner's *Philosophy of Freedom*, but this also requires an awakening to the full moral world that lives in the ground of thinking. The Other thinks in me. There is a totally new life that opens up, when one truly experiences the spiritually free I, weaving together with the angelic hierarchies in being thought by them, as one is morally connected

---

consciousness of a subject, to pure thematizing intentionality. Contrary to the ideas according to which thinking progressively seizes the world, which are always on the level of the 'intentional object', the *ideatum* and the grasp, the idea of the Infinite would contain more than it is capable of containing, more than its capacity as a *cogito*. The idea of the Infinite would somehow think beyond what it thinks. In its relation to what should be its 'intentional correlate,' it would be thrown off course, not resulting in anything or arriving at an end, and precisely not arriving at the finite, at a term or close. Certainly it is necessary to distinguish between, on the one hand, the pure failure of the nonachievement of an intentional aim which would still be ruled by a finality and, on the other hand, the deportation or the transcendence beyond any end and any finality: the thinking of the absolute without this absolute being reached as an end, which again would have signified finality and finitude. The idea of the Infinite is a thought released from consciousness, not according to the negative concept of the unconscious but according to the thought, perhaps the most profoundly considered thought, of the release with regard to being, of dis-inter-est: a relation without hold on being and without subservience to the *conatus essendi*, contrary to knowledge and perception. Concretely, this does not become some sort of modification of vision as a pure negative abstraction, but is accomplished ethically as a relation to the other human being." Levinas, *Basic Philosophical Writings*, pp 156-157

and ruptured in the heart and will by the otherness of the spirit-blood and spirit-fire. In real Anthroposophical practice, Christ begins to live as the spirit in my heart. Husserl would have to go one more step in order to see that the mute silence and the pure flow of time and consciousness that he perceives as the limit of his intuition is actually a shell that is experienced from the inside. His feelers can only touch the inner surface of this shell, like a chick poking around inside its egg. We could ask the question – why is it not possible to cross directly over the chasm and outside this shell by phenomenological intuition, or by Bergson's work on duration, or by simply wanting to do so? Why is there a threshold at all?

The sober truth is revealed in Steiner's works in many different ways. It hinges on the fact that our ordinary consciousness is more or less weak and immoral to the core. Our subjectivity is built on the moral activity of rejecting the Christ-spirit, the loving I, at each minute. But this means that I also reject each and every other person (in an earthly and a spiritual sense) at each minute as well. There are fallen spirits who are woven into my being on earth, and I must become conscious of them and begin to transform them before I can be an effective human living on earth and in heaven simultaneously. If I were allowed to just stroll right over into the spiritual worlds, I would just carry and pour evil, hatred, and selfish destruction into every corner. Ahriman, Lucifer, and the Anti-Christ would use my half-conscious subjectivity to attack the heavens. But true spiritual experience must be free. My earthly consciousness is to a very large degree only an ahrimanic/luciferic product. It requires tremendous moral growth to develop into kind of being that can enter the real spiritual world with the humble light of goodness, truth, and love that is appropriate to meet and work with the spiritual beings that live there. This requires a resilient and loving gentleness, not power, desire, and intellect. One must see one's evil nature in all objectivity from the outside before entering across the threshold. Husserl was simply not able to do this, if he even understood that it was possible. Steiner was able to do this, and several other of his students have now followed him across in the razor thin Anthroposophical way. Of course, the activity of letting the gentle words of the etheric Christ to live in your mouth, and resound in your heart, as He shows you how to become a spiritual human on the earth, has little to do with combining Rudolf Steiner quotes in new books made up of newly killed mental pictures. This is just more murder of the spirit. Dead secondary literature produces 100,000 new crucifixions. This fact is just not sufficiently noticed in what is falsely called 'spiritual research.'

One can only answer Husserl's writings (speaking to him in the spiritual world is a different matter), by saying – one must truly allow all of one's hopes and dreams of an immortal transcendental I die before praying for resurrection from the spiritual world and all of its beings. One must be awakened out of the powerlessness of infinite death, where the mute stupefaction rises to new intensity, and duration is

247

exploded by the void. Only Christ can awaken us here, which means the I AM of all truly transcendental selves. The etheric Christ, who shows us, as a resurrection experience, in head, heart, limbs, expanding and breathing out in stars, planets, and earth – how to become who we truly are in the depths of our being, is in sharp contrast to the anti-God that we created out of our little ego on earth. But in the purifying fire of this infinite shame of immorality, when it is gazed upon by the fury and living thunder of the hierarchies, is carefully transformed into a gentle light and a new moral life, which shows us how this evil can now be transformed by earthly-heavenly work, into goodness. Ahriman in us is burnt by the fire of Christ's love in my heart, and Lucifer must be transformed when he finds that true love can live outside of his narrow self-love, as Ben-Aharon has taught us. But don't worry - this is a long-term project! Through this resurrection, we can now look back at the Husserlian project and see that it was a minor planet with its constellations that were painted from the inside. He was a fine human being, and an astounding thinker, who struggled to find the truth every day, but ultimately, he painted a lifetime of work inside the eggshell. Now, we who are people of the future, working with the whole spiritual world, and the Christ spirit and the new time Spirit, can gently and kindly open this bubble and let it bear fruit in the spiritual world. His dead thoughts woven into the world ether, can be sprouted into new life. This can only happen if we can carry his work from the point of his death in 1938, through the abyss of the Holocaust, and into our own future. This means in the

248

spiritual sense that I recognize that I am ethically woven together and co-responsible for every being. In this way Husserl's highest work is carried to all places by the spiritual wind, like the floating seeds of the dandelion, as they are blown away into individual regions, leaving their dead parent behind. Husserl's Real Spirit was immortal, and his dead thoughts about the little 'transcendental ego' can also now rise from the grave. Now they can grow in a thousand new ways.

Chapter 11 – The Metamorphosis of Judgments Past: from Husserl's States of Affairs to the Spiritual World

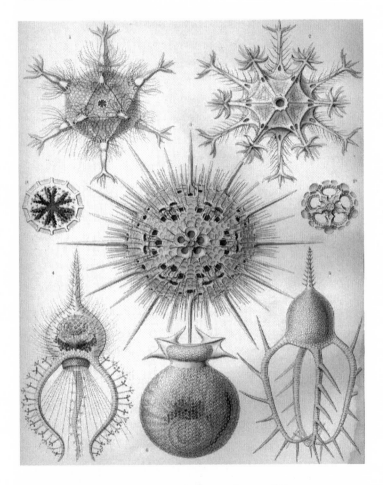

Phaeodaria from Haeckel's *Artforms of Nature*

How do we contain the solutions to the problems that we have already solved in all of our future thought about them? What are the connections that allow a previous idea to link up with new ideas? How can we expand a series of thoughts in the future without being overwhelmed by all of the details of our past thoughts about them? In *Formal and Transcendental Logic* and in *Experience and Judgment*, Husserl penetrates to the eidetic vision of higher forms of collections or syntheses of judgments, which he calls 'states of affairs' (*Sachverhalten* – 'the way that things are currently held together'). I would like to focus just on this element in this chapter.

The state of affairs in Husserl's sense does not mean the way that my children's toys are currently spread around the room, as I perceive them visually. These perceptual contents of current sense data as they contribute to the understanding of the whole sensible situation in the natural attitude is what Husserl calls the 'situation at present' (*Sachlage*). I have to shift to viewing my own thinking as it is unfolding itself moment by moment and creating thoughts if I am to investigate collections of previous judgments. The viewing of flexible sets of conclusions that have been created by logical thinking takes place inside the phenomenological reduction. I must view only the meaning content and its forms in the pure thinking sphere to find the Husserlian *Sachverhalten*.

Let us work with an example. Imagine that we are investigating lead (Pb) poisoning in animals. The literature suggests that dogs and cattle are also susceptible to lead poisoning, and not only the endangered California Condor. All of the ways that animals can ingest lead, from eating carrion killed with lead bullets, to eating paint chips and vegetation contaminated with the leakage from old batteries could be considered. This complex topic could result in me making the decision or judgment that the use of lead should be banned altogether. The element that we need to focus on here is how all of the facts about lead poisoning and many different animals are displayed when they are intuited on the concept plane itself. Of course, the real welfare of animals is ethically important, but that is not the element that we are considering now. What happens in thinking when I combine the concepts of dog, cow, and vulture into one set? How does a set or a collection of previous logical thought (with all of its sub-judgments, arguments, facts, and associations) appear and function when I see its essential and highest level in pure thinking? How do all of the details disappear from consciousness but still allow its essence to be taken up, worked over, and extended in the future? How does this complex ball of thought appear to intuition?

Husserl notes the strange fact that everything we have thought about the problem of lead-poisoning in various animals can also appear later on, right where we left them, as sources for further judgments. They have been actively created and then disappear from consciousness, but then reappear in a way (when we want to think about them again) that seems to be passively constituted. In following this through, we have to directly view the logical prototypes in a transcendental analysis proper. This also means that we have to investigate the fluctuating streams in the irreal life force matrix (the provisional concept plane and its cosmic and earthly context interwoven with living light, warmth and tone). How are larger complexes of the proto-types different from the local judgment as we encounter them in the foreground and the background in the multiple layers of noema and categorical essence (or living concept)? What are the organic and inorganic stages of transformation that we dive into in intuitive thinking?

Furthermore, if we are to cross over the gap between transcendental phenomenology and anthroposophy by diving down into a renewal and a creation of the moral life of the heart, are we prepared to maintain our consciousness as we enter the true fields of life, and indeed meet forces and spirits of every sort? This is the question for the spiritual scientific researcher who is following in Steiner's footsteps. If we are to fully enter into the world of flowing life, the elemental world proper, this means that a penetration into the true states of affairs would require (as we know from Steiner) a thorough description of the beings of the elements (gnomes, undines, sylphs, and salamanders) and their role in the etheric processes of thought, memory, and growth. The grid and the concept plane, which may first appear like the colored lines of a Kandinsky painting, eventually must be bypassed, when one crosses the threshold to meet one's moral connection to the whole world, which means to all other beings. To cross beyond Husserl's activity as he digs in the mines of linguistic concepts and pure logic-gems, let us study this statement from Steiner:

> States of consciousness can lie in all four forms of the physical plane [mineral, water, air, warmth] while the body of such an [elemental] being lies in the astral. We must think of the consciousness [of such an elemental being] in the solid Earth, the body in the astral; or a being that has its consciousness in the water and its body in the astral; then such a being with its consciousness in the air and its body in the astral and one with its consciousness in fire and its body in the astral. Present-day man knows but little of such beings; in our time it is only through poetry that they are known. Miners (of minerals) however know such beings very well. A gnome is only visible to someone who can see on the astral plane, but miners frequently possess such an astral vision; they know that gnomes are realities. Thus, on our Earth there exist various forms of consciousness, and what the natural scientist today calls laws of nature are the thoughts of beings who think on the physical plane but have their bodies on the astral plane. When in physics we have to do with laws of nature we can say: these are the thoughts of a being who has its body on the astral plane. The

forces of nature are creative beings and natural laws are their thoughts.[126]

This means that to penetrate into the realization of Truth, we have to extend our investigations in two dimensions: not only do we have to **1)** penetrate to the spiritual being active in lead to comprehend the issue of lead poisoning, we also have to **2)** penetrate to an Imaginative perception of the role of the elemental spirits in the process of thinking inside the elements of my head and body while I am investigating categories in the phenomenological reduction state of consciousness. The mineral element and the liquid element in my head and my whole body, for example, operate according to the creative activities of the elemental spirits. They are everywhere in me.

We also need to consider the parents of these elemental spirits, the angels proper. Steiner explains that not only do the angels live in our thinking, but that their sphere of activity on the earth is in the human brain itself. What is more, the elements that seem to be passively constituted in memory and in past thought forms is the result of the activity of the 3rd angelic hierarchy. Steiner says, "Just as we bear our own human Ego actually only in the outermost lobes of the brain, so do we bear the Angeloi, Archangeloi, etc. immediately beneath this region; yet still within

---

[126] GA 93a, 1905. This volume of lectures seems to contain rough notes and overviews of Steiner's actual words, rather than the high-quality stenographic reports that are found in many of the later lectures. Nevertheless, they are useful and filled with life.

the organisation of the head. There is the scene of their activities on earth; there are the starting-points of their activity...The Third Hierarchy, Angeloi, Archangeloi, etc. — concern themselves with that which has its physical organization in the human head, i.e. with our thinking. If they were not concerning themselves with our thinking — with that which is going on in our head — we should have no memory in ordinary earthly life. For it is the Beings of this Hierarchy who preserve in us the impulses which we receive with our perceptions. They are underlying the activity which reveals itself in our memory; they lead us through our earthly life in this first sub-conscious, or unconscious, region."[127]

When we cross the threshold beyond the bubble of phenomenological analysis into the living world of thought and life outside the body through moral intuition, we find the following. Spirit-Logic is made of fiery warmth, in so far as it is built up of the cosmic will, becoming human reason, as it adapts itself to the configuration of the human organs. When the spiritual-self awakens inside the Spirit Logic of the cosmos, living outside the body in the sacrificial world-warmth, streaming around to the greatest distances and heights and depths, - the warmth of the world-speech, made by beings who communicate from the spirit world itself are ringing out. In these moments, we discover that the meaning of the Cosmos is much different than what we combine into our little earthly logic. To find it, we have to pass through

---

[127]*Karmic Relationships* (GA 235) Vol 1, p 104-105

meaninglessness and nihilism. The paradox of the swell of meaninglessness that lives in Heller's *Catch-22*, for example, begins to surface, and all of the impossible tangents and chaos of Pynchon's *Gravity's Rainbow* are discovered to be an underlying feature of the full world reality. Yet, it is reasonable and healthy to be able to tranquilly create a humble and individual human meaning out of the lively chaos. The highest spiritual light coming from the I-AM can weave in this chaos, and a new creative meaning arises, coming from the builders of the future.

Back at the level of the connectivity of the ideal planes of thinking, it is necessary to describe and emphasize the fact that the airy-image smear that flows through the growth principles in the formative force substance displays the quality of continual shift and metamorphosis of form. Although the meaning forms penetrate into this sphere from higher unconscious spheres, and thus are passively constituted, the etheric forms of creative logical relationship between, for example, this individual fig plant, and the category of all plants proceeds in a floating, wispy, resonance that is like playing in an open pool of water. One can also note that an element or aspect of this imaginative substance (that is nonetheless effective, filled with force, alive and real) is particularly associated with the individual plant itself, while the rays of the will that shoot in a more linear fashion through this wafting light force can transmute or grasp and play with the elements of this substance that are associated with the human being in a more direct manner. We might say there is a localized passive imagination affecting the flow of sap in the individual plant and an active and expansive imagination substance waving and fluctuating in spiritual streams of possibility inside the human sphere (all of this investigation must, of course, be balanced out each time and brought into the moral wound of the heart, in order to look baldly at all of the selfish and vain implications of philosophical meandering. The real history of the earth, the riddle of evil and the nature of my own immoral nature must always be kept in mind in every spiritual investigation. The whole of humanity must always be in my heart's blood in every trip to the other side of threshold).

If we consider the spiritual and soul side of the issue, which means the way that my thinking, feeling, and willing is woven together with beings of warmth, light, air, liquid, density, love, wisdom, and so on, and then return to Husserl's statements, we can see more precisely how he was able to grasp an element of this life and bring it into consciousness, although inside the dying forms of the ahrimanic-luciferic bubble of the personal soul body. If we look back at his lively accomplishments, from the side of the spiritual love that lives in the free spiritual I, interpenetrated by the etheric Son of Man, then we can see the whole pulsing life of the entire nature of human and cosmic knowledge. It is hard to express publicly any words which show what this means – it is the warmth and light of a spiritual love that works in from the sun to the earth, and then back out to the sun once again. The I in the sun lives inside the heart of man, and the

258

spiritualizing blood of morality must now pulse inside human knowledge. Phenomenology without spirituality is dead and can only lead into the empty abyss. We can transform it and resurrect it, however, through our own consciousness and love.

Let us return to the mineralized thinking of Husserl as he mines calcified judgment forms inside the head. He picks up a coherent and detailed reflection in the consciousness soul of what happens in the spirit-self beyond the threshold. On one level, he perceives that he is moving into a new territory when he dives into the living flux of the plane and suction forces of the vast interlinking of categories in the ocean of thinking. We should mention that Lotze had already discussed the role of states of affairs (*Sachverhalten*) in his 3 books on Logic. But Husserl attempts to penetrate more deeply into the creation, solidification, disappearance, and future evolution of these higher-level judgment forms. For example, he calls paragraph 58 of *Experience and Judgment*, "Transition to a new level of predicative operations. The preconstitution of the state of affairs (*Sachverhalt*) as categorial objectivity and its 'eduction' (*Entnehmen*) by substantivation." In other words, Husserl notices that we enter a new region on the concept plane, when we see that previous groups of thought-forms are already there when we get there. But he also notes that we can extract part of their meaning essence in a new series of thoughts, and this leads to a new process of solidifying them. I cut out a new channel where the inference can flow, but the liquid comes from previous judgements, and the new channel leaves a remnant in the thought-plane. Husserl relates the whole process of progressing from a simple judgment to a 'state of affairs' like this:

> Up to now we have pursued the genesis of the proliferation of formations which can be constituted around a judgment of the simplest form, the original cell of the thematic connection of determination. We conceived of these forms as arising, as actually proceeding and continuously developing in a judicative process. But once such a cell has been constituted...then the judgment need not be discarded as soon as it is completely constituted in actual becoming...on the contrary, since every step of judgment represents a production of sense enclosed in itself, one can also build further on this operation itself. Just as it fades away in retention and is yet preserved, it is possible to continue by linking on it...It has lost its form as an independent proposition and now presents itself as a substrate in a new judgment. This naturally presupposes that the proposition has been substantified. This proposition, previously multi-rayed, and constituted in an original two-membered synthesis of determination, is now apprehended in a single ray...When in an act of judgment, one links on to a past judgment, this past judgment is therefore treated exactly as any substrate that enters into a predicative judgment as a subject...This implies that it must have been preconstituted as such and that this is the function of the preceding judgment. Accordingly, this function has, so to speak, a double face: in each step of judgment not only does a determination...of the substrate, originally pregiven and already

receptively apprehended, take place, not only is this substrate predicatively intended in an ever new way and invested with logical sense, but at the same time a new kind of objectivity is preconstituted: the state of affairs (*Sachverhalt*) 'S is p,' which is produced in a creative spontaneity.[128]

But we can carry the extract of this over into the virtual life fields of the etheric new earth. We plant new human seed thoughts in a soil of inspired life. We weave together, humans along with spiritual beings, each of us singing our own part in a cosmic chorus, as we tie each dying thought across the moral threshold, to grow new vines from the world of the dead in our calcium and limestone heads, into the seeds of the etheric earth. This is not imaginary, but an actual process, of what Yeshayahu Ben-Aharon calls cosmic-earthly husbandry – a new Eventful artform. The formal language that Husserl uses can be applied to all of the meaning-creating-experiences from the spiritual world through the astral and etheric worlds and on into the process of physical thought. This means that the spiritual I-Am learns how to create concepts in every plane. This provides, on the one hand, the universality of the Husserlian logical approach, but also undermines a clear distinction between the varieties of physical, etheric, soul, and spiritual levels. However, we can follow one very clear differentiation between the actively analyzed proposition that we followed through etherically : this fig plant belongs to the class of all plants, with its

---

[128] EJ p 237-8 [pgh 58]

corresponding flowing structures in the imaginative sphere to the next higher stage in which this analyzed thought-formation becomes organically combined with a higher possible judgment about this earlier judgment. It becomes absolutely evident to the phenomenological researcher that this 'state of affairs' (we could call it a *concept-seedling* or an '*omim*' to escape from the deadness of English) has a certain liveliness in the head sphere and beyond, flowing and twisting as an invisible form of calcifying protoplasm in the personal soul body. To contrast it with the archetypal plant of Goethe, Husserl's state of affairs is not a complete spiritual Imagination, because it does not involve the life of the whole human, but is a rather narrow accomplishment that is incarnated strongly in the head sphere. Yet it is not illusory, and through moral intuition, we can now connect it to the spiritual earth across the threshold, to nourish spirit earthly fields. We spread this energized thought-crushed limestone onto our spiritual fields to fertilize spiritualized thought, and to aid the Michaelic spirits in resurrecting human science. Husserl continues -

> However, for the substantivation in which the state of affairs is educed from a judgment, so that it henceforth functions as a substantive in a new judgment, there is nothing analogous at the lower level. The object which here becomes the subject in a new judgment is nothing which could also be apprehended in a simple receptivity; rather, it is an object of an entirely new kind, a result of the judicative operation of predication, which could occur only in the upper level of predicative spontaneity. Consequently, in reference to their

262

origin, we call such objects syntactical or categorical objectivities...they have a kind of inner life and an independence with regard to the lower level.[129]

What does this mean? For the spiritual researcher engaged in spiritualizing transcendental phenomenology, it becomes clear that one has to continuously split the consciousness into two zones – entering into everyday consciousness to think through Husserl in the precise region where he operates, and then cross outside the body and look back, to cooperate with the spiritual self, and the helpful spiritual co-workers, to investigate and balance out the work. We are performing at the same time, a soul and spiritual e-duction or extraction into the new Event-filled life world where the Michael School is working. From the phenomenological zone, there are several approaches that could be taken in investigating these categorical objectivities in the sphere of the directly viewable transformations of meaning-elements in thinking. First, it is possible that people can communicate with one another while the part of themselves which swims in universal thinking, can open the way to a mutual understanding of the concept-powers that are acting in a certain situation. On the other hand, it must always be remembered that these living transformations of concept-events and powers, these meaning-events, are not perceived

---

[129] EJ p 239

263

outwardly like color, textures, position, and other natural processes. All of the investigation in this text must be based on the capacity to see thinking intuitively.

It also should be remembered that 'syntactical' is used in a phenomenological or logical way to refer to combinations of intuited thought forms that are pre-linguistic and not to their formulations in any particular language. There is a glue in the constellations on the virtual plane or non-actualized encyclopedia, and the new geographies and combinations on the proto-matrix of meaning may be hinted at with a written alphabet, but only if the reader is able to then use the letter combinations to access the virtual encyclopedic demonstrations of terrain directly again. Syntax is like the short-term memory of what happens in the multiple constellations of virtual flux on the planes. In the moral zone, the syntax becomes the 'xyntax' of the rhizome of the blood pumping through new spiritual human communities.

That means in one sense, syntax (the syntagmatic feature in logic) is the joining of the essence of spirit-words, into new strands of event-meaning, when the speech of the essence of meaning is revealed anew each time, from spirit-creativity. But these spirit word-streams of life criss-cross the thought-forming virtual encyclopedia, coming from different dimensions that can be traced, but which are not part of the surface or the interior of the conceptual plane itself. And the open door of the heart in the world must pulse through, maintaining the center. Husserl would

264

say that in the construction of larger strings of reasoning and complex ideas from smaller elements, one is not merely using linguistic rules or abstracting from sense events of cause and effect, but rather the syntagmatic joining of thinking is a meeting of real essences. These larger shifting forms, become like flashing light balls, or twisting and rolling husks of chestnuts, when looked at in the human soul body. If we understand the deeper implications of the connections of logical thinking, we see that each book that is seen with the eyes, points to an invisible book that is read with the capacity of the human to swim in universal thought events. A secondary problem lies in being able to then see the boundary between one's own mental representations of these happenings on the virtual blockchain, and opening up one's soul to the outside, beyond one's personal connection to this terrain. This is beyond where Husserl was able to penetrate. In this move, the spiritual I awakens in the midst of the world of idea-events and idea-happenings and one is living in a new sphere altogether. The moral reality and effects of each thought is understood now, and the heart and will is involved in a wide-spread cosmic process outside the memory of the human body. But the connection with normal human consciousness is maintained. The spiritual happenings of the moral states of affairs or Sachverhalten are led by the human spiritual I which invites the spiritual beings at the bottom of each concept to meet and cooperate in a ceremony of moral knowledge. This ceremony is an invitation and does not depend on the subjective wants of the individual human, but it would be a coworking with other spirits.

In this way, we see that normal thinking which supposes that any combination is possible is a rather aggressive, immoral, sewing together of a variety of corpses and skins that one stores in linear skeins of abstraction in the subjective thinking sphere, and then in neurological connections inside the totally dead nervous system.

If one remains inside the subjective or narrow view of personal representational thinking, one may even come to a viewing of non-sensible forms arising during personal thought. These shapes that Husserl obviously saw with clarity in the eidetic reduction are not universal, or spiritually moral. These higher-level deposits of previous conclusions are almost like spheres of fluctuating light with individual needles coming out of them on all sides, comparable to the covering over chestnuts. In fact, they look quite a bit like the intricate sea creatures that Haeckel illustrated, especially the large central form of the *Phaeodaria* at the beginning of this chapter. There is a remarkable similarity between these eidetic forms seen in phenomenological intuition and the wide variety of marine life that Haeckel illustrated. There is presumably a hidden connection in their development, but I have not yet perceived it consciously in 'the lab.'

These syntagmatic organelles of meaning-substances can then make attachments of sense through the diverse 'needles' that extend livingly on all sides, in every meaningful direction. The further logical combinations into future judgments link up with their needles. These tubes carry the essence of

266

the wholeness of the previous thought, but in a condensation that flows out into the new region of the thought planes faster than immediately. This condensation fluid on the concept planes, is mirrored in two ways in lower regions – first, through the neurobiological growths in the brain, and then also in the process of logical continuation, which allows the flow of the willfully organized representations to take place at all in a rational wholeness. If the parts of the syllogism were disconnected as objects far from one another in the desert, then the knowledge process could not happen at all. The miracle of reason, connects the whole together, but in ways that the former conclusion or form becomes an extract, while the full saturation of the presently intuited thinking-web displays itself in a mode which has no distance from the temporary phosphorus of the self-reflective inner consciousness of subjectivity. The potential elements of future judgments are light and airy, while the past accretions become viscous and slow. They are temporary accumulations that hold seeds of earlier formations inside them in a way that can contribute and grow in future essential intuitions or direct perceptions with visionary eyes into layers of meaning.[130] One is even surprised that like natural

---

[130] Susan Bachelard in her unparalleled book, *A Study of Husserl's Logic*, is astute in pointing out the difference between categorial objectivities and syntagmatic (or syntactic) objectivities. The categories are grasped as individuals in intuition, while the syntagmatic objects are produced by the collective activity of judgment and organization in the process of creative thought. See pp 77-79

fields, one may return several years later to the same moment in the logical process, and find that something has grown in the meantime – a life plant of essential possible knowledge can arise from the new joint, the new articulation. It lives in our personal web of light and it can be viewed from the outside in with the part of the astral body and the I AM which lives outside the body, as Steiner explains.

But if these flexible memory seeds and husks are mistaken for the real impersonal and objective happenings in the spiritual world, filled with morality through and through, this can cause many false understandings. The ahrimanic spirit that lives in our soul tries to maintain the seeds and husks as hardened forms in the personal soul body. On the other side, one can try to carry the personal and subjective view into the visionary, without the sense of morality and without the awakening of the full spiritual I (which is capable of incarnating and excarnating). The luciferic spirit in us takes the light element in the seeds and flies away into personal bliss, leaving the husks behind. There is always a war taking place in the etheric fields of the new earth. The living element in these chestnut light forms could be called *Tsimo-bizi*, in the forms they take that are of use for the luciferic spirits that wish to spark right off into the high heavens of the world. But the New Event allows us to do something else with it. This ecstatic light form can be brought down into the body, to die in the blood of the heart and one can patiently wait for spirit resurrection, if the spirit world wills it. Of course, the other side of the issue, is when the thought-sludge

268

becomes so dense in front of the head, that it solidifies and traps you back into the ahrimanic solid world-view.[131] These are the difficulties that arise when one is trying to contribute to the creation of a new etheric body, beginning from the logical forms discussed in transcendental phenomenology. Work with the pure percepts, sensations, and colors of nature can provide the necessary balance, if one is using phenomenology as a way to spiritualize the thinking pole.

Thus, we have a very complicated situation happening when one collects or joins together a variety of categories into a large thought which attempts to understand a larger situation as a whole. We have subjective and objective, illusory and real situations of affairs (*Sachlage*) in the sensible givens; phosphoric soul light, *Tsimo-bizi*, real categorial sets that are intuited but still within the subjective part of the soul, and we have the reflections taking place inside the nervous system and brain itself. Where do

---

[131] Ben-Aharon discussed this in some of his blog posts from 2011, "Brentano and Husserl...were striving for a fully conscious, scientific approach to spiritual reality by means of developing, as powerfully as possible, the soul and cognitive power that brings man deeper into his physical incarnation and embodiment. And spiritual science is created in each moment in which we are able to strengthen this power – as they did – but in order to use the strength thus gained in order to reverse intentionality's natural course and essence. Neither thinker could see through this paradox and therefore both believed that what was needed...is to develop intentionality much stronger and further. But this is a real illusion. Precisely the reverse is true."

we find our way out of this labyrinth? One can perform the active forgetfulness and the devotion, to dissolve the whole crystal structure. Then morally, while recognizing and admitting your evil nature and potential, wait for the spirit widths of spirit love of Christ to speak and will into you, to bring increasing wakefulness to the half-zombie consciousness of earthly beings in the 21st century. I hear the call of the Lord as I am bound in the cloth and the darkness like Lazarus. But now my higher Self must also love what is morally corrupt in me, devoting its work to changing my vices into virtues. Christ now teaches me to freely awaken my self, through my Self, in a fully modern way, progressing one step beyond the initiation of Lazarus.

But which light shines from the outside of the tomb? One can be deceived when one's own soul light is taken as a substance which the luciferic spirits intensify and lead on, but without the individual I of the human being remaining spiritually awake and recognizing the world karmic happenings and moral reversals, betrayals, and unconsciousness which arise through representational thinking. Ecstatic forms in the interior eye are not yet seen as spiritual beings on this side of the threshold. Or if they appear as such on the fabric of the grid or the hyperbolas, they are not real. Only when one has crossed over in the drama of self-knowledge and devotion to the truth of the spirit, can one see the larger spiritual context in which my soul gains knowledge, creates ideas and makes strings of inference. When I am seen by the Christ, I must differentiate his light from Lucifer's, and I must know

270

myself as both the seen, and the seer. I must also see
with gentle objectivity my never-ending mendacity.

Now, we must advance into the real spiritual
world, by looking outside of the head, and down into
the limbs and the periphery of the limbs, into the
turbulence of the warmth and chaos, out in the
distances of oneself, where one is a stranger to oneself,
and then beyond to what is distinctly human. This
threefold unity of human essence, is penetrated by the
upright standing I, capable of living and dying in any
situation of harmony or disharmony, as far as the
source of its I-AM-ness is felt to be the free gift of the
World-I or Christ. All of the too bright elements of the
luciferic inwardness can be de-actualized, and deflated
to give an entrance to the event-terrain. Lucifer's first
light of dawn gives way to the higher empty light of
the Invisible Sun.[132] At this point we understand that
the categorial *Sachverhalten* are really the present
coordination of the interaction of spiritual beings with
one another, and with the soul and spirit constitution
of the human at this moment. Steiner says, "When you
are in this world of living and weaving thoughts, you
are in the hierarchy of angels," and "There, ideals are
living beings of the hierarchy of angels and flow
through spiritual space, looking at us with warmth."[133]
Thus, the luciferic phosphorus can be calmed down in
the heart's warmth, where the judgment forms

---

[132] The tendencies of the proto-plasmic judgment husks to
become Tzimo-bizi is calmed down to become O-Mim.
[133] *The Presence of the Dead on the Spiritual Path*, pp
59-60

become trans-valuated gold. Here, the silent breeze that blows the clouds of soul and spirit light creates a new human spirit element – [Blood-Diamond-Gold] = [   ].

Let us return now from this window of infinite light back down into the eidetic seeing of meaning in Husserl's realm. By returning and leaving again, we are performing an earthly-cosmic stitching of life substance. The stars breathe into the earth, the earth erupts into the stars. The sun kneads into the soil, the lava becomes karmic planetary causal streams in space. Even the smallest thought, feeling, and act can join this new conscious pulse. Regarding these judicative states of affairs, Husserl says elsewhere:

> In the transformation that takes place by drawing the conclusions of manifold judicative activities in relation to the momentary, present determination-themes into the new judgment that is being carried out, the state-of-affairs, the intended meaning in the first sense, remains untouched.[134]

This is a subtle and brilliant finding, because it shows us how, in the flow of rigorous thinking, we may return to the former fully saturated knowledge moment, and then rework the whole process without losing the former meaning conclusions. In this move, we allow the former judicative manifold to retreat. It is de-saturated. Yet it remains fully functional and applicable to current states of thinking, even though

---

[134] APAS p 336

we are allowing it to fade into the past, while we are bringing other elements to the fore in the distance-less saturation of thinking-viewing. The angels take over its substance, in caring for human life-memory tapestries. It leaves our consciousness. But to return to the past conclusion, and to re-work the thought-lineage is like thinking backwards, while intuitively viewing the memory fabric. We re-saturate it, which means that we forget the angels and weave again in our dying pictures. And indeed, it is very productive and educational for the spiritual scientific researcher to rewind and live through the virtual encyclopedia plane backwards. The connectivity that Isis-Madonna-Demeter-Rhea-Nut weave can be opened to understanding in new ways by living through meaning backwards.

Yet, we must remember the post-structuralists' findings here, which teach us that we must also always pay attention to the living, pulsing forgotten periphery, which is also connected to the extracted moments of adjudicative intuitive processes. This is also a wonderful discovery, because the frozen kernel is still left, and the image from the original extract, but when it is nourished again by the whole world, the entire thought process can blossom, develop, expand into new life and the whole is renewed. The multiple levels of devoted erasure, lead us to deeper and deeper arche-traces, if we apply Derrida's technique along with Steiner's here. All knowledge and indeed all reality of human and world is given the incredible gift of renewal here. Man himself is not erased, like Foucault's face in the sand, but he changes into new forms, and creates new communities, with a rich spiritual brotherhood. These are free individuals joined together by spiritual care rather than by blood or soil. But harsh battles are waged, on earth and in worlds above and below. We slowly create new acts of freedom out of old habits.

We must keep alive a dual half-frozen, half melted derivate of previous thinking. Yes, we need to locate the conclusion and the sets of previous rational lines of thought, but each seed must be both solid enough to build on, flexible and alive enough to grow another connection, and also empty enough to be filled in from the other soul and spiritual side. But that is totally or virtually possible. The current state of logical affairs at time T must remain volatile and filled with cosmic extractive warmth. It is quite important to discover and create multiple ways of freeing the inner essences of thoughts from their attachment to particular linguistic forms or specific relationships to images, memories, or hardened collections of judgments. To open the cages of words to free the living spirits of meaning from their incarceration, is to strive for that universal, cosmopolitan, inner consciousness-fire and grammar-life that is an essential feature of the modern procedure of spiritual growth under the influence of the Spirit of Time, Michael. For example, the old name for Latin, 'Grammatica,' now can be consciously resurrected from the dead side of human thinking. We can stand humbly in the presence of the new evolution of the Spirit of Grammar and Syntax, as she stands in Heaven. And we wake up, as she is freed, which

means that we remember what we have forgotten.
Steiner says:

> So long as we only clothe our knowledge in these
> languages, and do not carry it right up into the
> thoughts, we cannot come near Michael...We only
> come to Michael when we get through the words
> to real inner experiences of the Spirit – when we
> do not hang on the words, but arrive at real inner
> experiences of the Spirit. This is the very essence,
> the secret of modern initiation: to get beyond the
> words, to a living experience of the
> Spiritual...Precisely when we no longer think in
> language, we begin to feel it.[135]

---

[135] GA 233a

Conclusion - The Limits of Husserlian Phenomenology & Some Little Keys

After a certain stage of spiritual and soul development following the path of spiritual science, one can begin to see the limits of the Husserlian project more clearly and accurately. The whole issue at the center of his phenomenological discoveries and struggles lie in the extent to which concepts can be directly seen in the mind's eye. They certainly can be, as I and a growing number of others can confirm from direct experience, no matter how much people misunderstand or misinterpret the noematic-noetic realm described by Husserl. But is the seeing of concepts the fulfillment and the end of the process of knowledge itself? No. His partial success lies in widening the field of idealism, which can allow the student of Husserl to view the realm of concepts and elaborate their features and contours which are themselves neither dependent on their relationship to sensible objects, nor merely associative or inferential strings of reason. But in addition, the Husserlian self-evident appearing of a new realm of experience in concepts, maintains at least two different functions that are essential for phenomenology to move beyond the older form of Platonism or the whole history of the visionary insight at the center of the development of Christian mysticism in the West.

First of all, Husserl penetrates to a certain degree beyond the visionary appearances of the concepts and categories themselves into the non-imagistic realm of their will-filled meaning life, grasped by the intuitive aspect of the understanding. This thoroughly penetrates the new region of conceptual-appearance with the logical and mathematical rigor applied to epistemological and scientific investigations. This maintains and secures the direct link between the reality of empirical investigation and progress and the conceptual creations that can provide the foundation for all rigorous science, in a modern and free way. In other words, it maintains a link with scientific objectivity and strict reason, that does not just fall into visionary or mystical obscurity and fantasy. Beholding pure concepts is no easy matter.

Secondly, the Husserlian phenomenological project is based on the will-filled activity of thinking fully controlled by a self-conscious I that witnesses its own activity. In this sense, a good deal of the fruits of Descartes, Kant, and Fichte are maintained, extended, and penetrated with self-conscious thinking activity, controlled by the I. In this way the projects of Platonism become intensely penetrated by the strong individualism brought to the fore by the task of the Hebrew people.[136] It is now the individual and free human who is at the root and self-subsistent free

---

[136] For more on this, see Ben-Aharon's *Jerusalem* (2019).

activity of the creation of knowledge, concepts, and earthly thinking. But now the self-conscious link to the true region of spiritual word and spiritual thinking must be self-consciously crafted by the individual work of humans. This is what Steiner's achieved in his life's work and his whole being, which still stands as a living prototype for each person to meet and independently develop. It is a living seed in the *Philosophy of Freedom*.

Husserl's phenomenology possesses the scientific and mathematical rigor that was not present in Plato, Bacon, Fichte, or even Brentano. He kept the door open to an independent conceptual reality that Frege wished to cut off entirely. In Husserl's phenomenology the activity of subjective thinking is intensified and extends to its height, but also reaches its limits. Therefore, in this sense, what is positive in Husserl's ego-centered elaboration of the drama of intentionality, is also the same thing which sets up a boundary which he himself was not able to pass. It is only Steiner who was really able to show how thinking can operate outside the limits of subjectivity without losing scientific rigor, objectivity, or diminishing the freedom and flexibility of the I. In this way the clarity and precision of modern consciousness, thinking, and perception can be maintained in the development of the new soul and spiritual senses. However, this turn to spiritual reality in Imagination, Inspiration, and Intuition in the specifically anthroposophical sense, is a giant step beyond Husserl. This fact is also not clearly understood. It is a giant step because the central meaning of all concepts shift considerably when the threshold to the spiritual world is consciously crossed. Furthermore, the moral import of the subject's relationship to the living world becomes a defining and essential feature, and indeed the reality of the spiritual beings who constitute the complete nature of the self and the world begin to appear to consciousness. This requires an immense resilience that has nothing to do with escaping from life. The transcendental I of Husserl is not yet the Spirit-Self that awakens during spiritual development. The noema is not yet a spiritual being, his Life-world is not the world of elementals. The intersubjective ponderings of Husserl's *Cartesian Meditations* are still mere subjective projections (and really the weakest part of his phenomenology).

Rudolf Steiner indicates that devotion to nature is essential to really enter into spiritual scientific investigation and research in his lectures on *Anthroposophy and Science* from 1921 (GA 324):

> One must, in fact, repeatedly resolve to intensify one's thinking ability, the force of one's inner soul work – to strengthen it through love of external nature. Otherwise one simply cannot proceed. One goes consciously into oneself, but again and again one is thrown back, and instead of what I would call an inner view, one gets something not right. One must overcome the inward counterblow that develops.[137]

I think we can be frank about the fact that in Husserl's work we find nothing of a serious love of

---

[137] GA 324 pp 110-111

external nature or heart-filled devotion as a counterbalance to the clarity of thinking developed there. He may have personally felt it, but it never influenced his phenomenology. His notes on ethics and value theory are traditional, theoretical, and merely external. It was only at the end of his life (1935) that he began to see that 'love in the truest sense is the greatest problem to be solved by phenomenology.'[138] But, although it can seem strange to those who have no experience in these matters, it is just this devotion, and love of the Otherness (of other humans, animals, plants, stones, stars, spiritual beings) that leads to progress outside our reversed soul bubble. If Husserl had truly allowed the 'Goethean mythology' to penetrate him further, he could have crossed the threshold into living thinking. If he had allowed his early important 'overpowering religious experiences' to light up the moral side of his phenomenology, or if he had tried to penetrate the religious experiences (which for him remains a private and not a professional and public affair), with phenomenological insight, he might have made it

---

[138] *"Liebe im echten Sinn ist eines der Hauptprobleme der Phänomenologie, und das nicht in der abstrakten Einzelheit und Vereinzelung, sondern als universalproblem – nach den intentionalen Elementarquellen und nach ihren enthüllten Formen der von den Tiefen zu den Höhen und universalen Weiten hervortreibenden und sich auswirkenden Intentionalität."* From *Problems at the Boundaries of Phenomenology: Analysis of the Unconscious, Instincts, Metaphysics, and Late Ethics,* 2015; translation mine. To consider Husserl's ethics from a purely external viewpoint, see Donohoe 2016, Bello 2018, Ferrarello 2015

through the wall of subjectivity.[139] But nevertheless, what he could not do, we ourselves can do today, and that is the most wonderful aspect about human progress. The spiritual and soul being of thinking Herself develops and unfolds over time, and we with Her. She becomes more and more filled with Self-understanding, and so do we in proportion to our devotion to the Truth. This is the cosmic beauty of the art of the self-revelation of human-cosmic knowledge. Steiner shows the complete picture of the method that is really necessary to enter into spiritual scientific research:

> We have already discussed Imagination and we know it does in fact relate to reality although at first it appears to have pictorial character. It relates to a reality, but at first, we have only pictures in our consciousness. When we experience Inspiration, we advance from the pictorial to the corresponding spiritual reality. When we reach the moment in which external sense perception is completely extinguished through Inspiration, a new content appears for the first time. The content that appears corresponds to our existence before conception...Thus this Imagination

---

[139] Husserl writes to his student Arnold Metzger in 1919 about his early years, "I still lived in an almost exclusive dedication to my theoretical work – even though the decisive influences, which drove me from mathematics to philosophy as my vocation, may lie in overpowering religious experiences and complete transformations. Indeed, the powerful effect of the *New Testament* on a 23-year-old gave rise to an impetus to discover the way to God and to a true life through a rigorous philosophical inquiry." Letter of 4 September, 1919

fills itself with a real spiritual content that represents our pre-birth existence. Characterized in this way, this may still seem paradoxical to many people of our time. One can only indicate the exact point in the cognitive process where such a view of the human soul-spiritual self enters in, and where what we call the question of immortality takes on real meaning. At the same time, we gain a more exact view of the other pole of the human organization. When we penetrate what we have at first only as intuitive belief and raise this to knowledge, the possibility arises to relate Imaginations – although in another way than in the case just described – to the conditions after death. In short, we have a view of what one can call the eternal in man and I will only just mention the following. When Intuition has developed further, to the point it is really capable of reaching, we develop our true I for the first time. And within the true I, there appears to inner vision what in anthroposophical spiritual science is referred to as knowledge of repeated earth-lives.[140]

Do you see the cosmic fields and living potential that is available for the advancement of humanity? I hope that the developments that were achieved and demonstrated in this book in every sentence can contribute to a widening of the doorway that leads to the redemption of the will, feeling, and thinking of humanity by a spiritual scientific path and the subsequent uplifting of all human life, creativity, culture and work. The doorway to the consciousness

---

[140] GA 324 p 122

of the eternal in you is now open, and if you do your side of the work, it can eventually dawn on you, no matter your failings. I have offered little keys here and there which can lead you to the Mothers, if you are willing to become the Mothers. But this means to be able to cross from atomic physics to the Void-voltage of Moral Fire. Try! We are all beginners.

Several of the **keys** that I have indicated or enacted in the book are as follows:

1. Find the difference between sense perception and categorial intuition.
2. Find the difference between a representation or mental image and an imageless concept. Create a new imageless concept.
3. Experience the difference between the noema and the essential meaning behind it. Pull this experience down into the heart with devotion.
4. Use imaginative variation to uncover the Idea behind the different species. Combine this with honest self-knowledge.
5. Actively develop devotion for Truth, Beauty, Goodness and a love for Nature; then peel, erase, and forget a meticulously formed mental image (and its concept) and wait in the Emptiness. Do not forget your I-AM however.
6. Working with other people, listen to and intimately follow their speaking,

thinking, and find their I-AM nature. Carefully locate the limits and potential in this.

7. Look honestly at your moral failings and social reversals as a stranger; experience the moral shock of the Other whom you have always ignored.

8. Activate the I-AM thinker who creates all concepts; it lives both inside and outside the body. How is the I-AM connected to the heart?

9. Differentiate between the dead etheric grid (the light forms active in mental representation) and the supersensible etheric, soul, and I-AM activity coming from outside of it.

10. Dissolve the dead representations with love and devotion in the heart.

11. Experience the moral shock of being cored out in the heart by the Other, after the fashion of Levinas.

12. Find the limits of representation by thinking about the end, thinking about death, and considering how everything physical will pass away. Instead of symbolically, make a moral-cognitive advancement through the first three degrees of Masonry.

13. Experience the will that acts in thinking both inside and outside the body; experience the It Thinks and the ocean of thought in which you swim. Create a

new Middle-I, who confronts while experiencing.

14. Awaken the Fichtean intuition; look to the center of the I-AM thinker, and with devotion, wait for the opening to the Spiritual World in the center of the I-AM.

15. Follow the pure percept into pure quality and moral meaning; follow the Goethean archetype to intensity and real spiritual Imagination.

Of course, these practices derive from Husserl and especially Steiner. Many of these ideas have been introduced and elaborated more fully in the schooling and in the books of Yeshayahu Ben-Aharon. I have practiced them all and demonstrated them in this book. Have fun and work together with other people! This work can no longer succeed if we work in isolation.

With this book, I hope to end the stage of my life dedicated to struggling with the mystery of Husserl's books. It has lasted 25 years. It is true that I barely touched upon some of his achievements. No matter. It is time to take off this jacket and hang it up. I honor his faithful and never-ending quest for truth and his clarity of consciousness, which attempted to penetrate into every sphere of human reality. I hope to continue to aspire to meet the true Spirit of Anthroposophy, and to follow the living guidance of Rudolf Steiner. I also hope to continue my own work in the future with the spiritualization and creation of new precise scientific and technical concepts, specifically in chemistry, which can contribute to the building of the new earthly-human sun. Christ will teach us how to become good spirit farmers. Let us learn together:

Those who know that the progress of mankind depends upon living apprehension of the mighty Event of Golgotha are they who as the "Masters of Wisdom and of the Harmony of Sensation" are united in the great Guiding Lodge of mankind. And as once the "tongues of fire" hovered down as a living symbol upon the company of the apostles, so does the "Holy Spirit" announced by Christ Himself reign as the Light over the Lodge of the Twelve. The Thirteenth is the Leader of the Lodge of the Twelve. The "Holy Spirit" is the mighty Teacher of those we name the "Masters of Wisdom and of the Harmony of Feelings". It is through them that his voice and his wisdom flow down to mankind in this or that stream upon the earth. The treasures of wisdom gathered together by the spiritual scientific movement in order to understand the universe and the Spirits therein, how through the "Holy Spirit" into the Lodge of the Twelve; and that is what will ultimately lead mankind step by step to free, self-conscious understanding of Christ and of the Event of Golgotha. Thus to 'cultivate' spiritual science means to understand that the Spirit has been sent into the world by Christ; the pursuit of spiritual science is implicit in true Christianity. This will become more and more evident to men; and then they will realize that in spiritual science they have a potent asset in their lives. Men owe to spiritual science the consciousness which dawns in them by degrees, that Christ is the Spirit Who fills the world with light. And the consequence will be that here on this earthly globe, in the physical world itself, men will make progress in their moral life, in their life of will, in their intellectual life. Through physical life itself the world will be spiritualized in ever-increasing measure. Men will grow in goodness, strength and wisdom and will gaze with ever deepening vision into the foundations and origins of existence. They will bear with them into the super-sensible life the fruits acquired in this physical life, and ever and again bring these fruits back from the super-sensible life into a new incarnation.

Rudolf Steiner (GA 107, 22 March 1909)

ENDNOTES –

[i] To follow our work here, you must 1) find a way to perceive that concepts that are present in individual lines of thought are not simply mental pictures that have been copied from sense experience and are now used in abstraction to refer in the present to concrete sensuous experience in the past. Sets of anything, the operations of Logic, Nostalgia, Love, Imagination, Angels, Ghosts, the mind's Eye, and Memory are all examples of concepts that are not wholly derived from sense objects or external physical experience. It is true that the imagination is a faculty, and that I must experience a faculty before I can create a suitable concept from meeting its essence. But the faculty of imagination is certainly not itself derived from sense experience, and thus neither is the concept of imagination, which is created by thinking activity. Love is not something I gather from sense experience. Some of us certainly perceive images as images in the mind's eye. This

was already proved in psychological studies in the 60s in the following way. A person who could see 'eidetic images' was given one half of a stereoscopic image at one time, and then the other half was shown to him later. The new object, which could only be perceived through uniting both elements of the stereoscopic image, in a visible manner, was definitively perceived by the subject in the mind's eye. 2) Furthermore, the reader must come to understand that a concept itself, although existing in its own realm, will never be seen with physical eyes. It is well known that others in the history of philosophy have denoted concepts like Space and the operations of Logic by the term '*a priori*,' meaning 'from what is prior to experience' and often indicating a logical or fundamental necessity. For example, if there were no fundamental concept of space beforehand, none of my sense perceptions could be related effectively to one another. Furthermore, if I am to think in a consistent manner that is understandable to others and if science is to progress, I must follow the rules of logic that are not themselves perceived in my sense experience. I could watch the functioning of a logic gate in a circuit which mimics one element of the Boolean algebra, but the understanding of its content and operation can only be thought. A priori elements must be present 'before' in some sense. In contrast, the term *a posteriori* has then been used to refer to knowledge that arises from actual sense experience. For example, I only understand the trajectories of actual bouncing balls after I have observed many of them. Certain physical laws can only be derived from thinking about data from sense perception. The laws of the physical world are not derived from the basic laws of logic or the mere idea of space. However, I will not use the terms a priori and a posteriori in this book, because the concept of **experience** is sufficiently expanded in phenomenological and spiritual scientific research to make these concepts at least vague and probably useless. Grasping the concept of 'glory' or a set in inner intuition is a sort of experience. A serious philosophical controversy surrounds the idea of what thinking and apriority really means. On one side,

288

there are those who conceive what is *a priori* to be merely **deducible** in critical reflection from the given evidence (Kant and the majority of natural scientists). I can rationally discover what conditions must undergird any possible experience of knowledge, but this camp says that I cannot actual perceive these conditions themselves in the way I perceive a tree. They are merely thought out in abstraction. On the other side, certain philosophers (like Plato, Hegel, Fichte, Husserl, Steiner, and Hicks) have directly experienced in a rigorous fashion that concepts and ideas are directly graspable as individual realities in **clear intuitive seeing** (whether or not Kant meant to use the distinction between a priori and a posteriori only to define the mode of verification required for a specific judgment, or to refer to the content of the judgment itself, is of no consequence to our investigation). Let us instead use terms of more clarity and less controversy. Of course, Husserl himself also seems to use the term 'a priori' in an equivocal manner, sometimes referring to a logical necessity determined independently of sense experience, and other times to indicate a quality of the realm of essences, or the objects revealed through intuition in the phenomenological reduction in a more general sense. Heidegger sometimes vacillates on this as well, as in his *Basic Problems of Phenomenology.*

ii I am not proposing that I agree with Brentano's viewpoint. Goethe, Husserl, Fichte, and Steiner would also look at things differently than Brentano. Nevertheless, Husserl expanded Brentano's notion of the 'intentional relation' into new territory in his phenomenological investigations. Certain philosophers who belong to the 'analytical tradition' would even dispute this interpretation of Brentano, but you can read more about that in various journals or books like Jaquette's *Cambridge Companion to Brentano* and Breazeale's *Fichte and the Phenomenological Tradition* (2010, De Gruyter, NY). It was my pleasure to study under Jaquette at Penn State in the 1990s. There was a ripe philosophical environment in State College at that time period, where I not only received an introduction to

Rudolf Steiner in a contemporary philosophy class led by Irene Harvey, but also was able to study Nietzsche and Derrida with Charles E. Scott and Medieval Philosophy with Joseph Kockelmans (who wrote among a vast collection of works, some of the earliest introductions to Husserl's work in English in the 1960s. He spoke at Heidegger's funeral and also liked to tell the story of sleeping in the same bed with Derrida at a conference where lodging was scarce. He said they 'slept together like brothers').

Made in the USA
Middletown, DE
02 November 2019